'Explains the motivations and frustrations of the conspirators ... a memorable short book, written in crisp prose' *Daily Express*

'Provides many insights ... detail abounds ... astonishing' *Daily Telegraph*

'[A] short, modest memoir ... celebrates a long-since vanished generation of scholar-warriors'
Daily Mail

'A fascinating description of some of the peripheral details of the plot as well as a unique account of the life of a cavalry officer' *The Tablet*

'A remarkable and honest testament to the courage of the small band of resisters who dared to try and stop Hitler and his lunacy' *News Letter*

'An invaluable testimony ... von Boeselager has produced an account infused with great honesty, a thousand miles from the standard accounts that sometimes appear in the newspapers' *Le Monde*

T0349218

Philipp Freiherr von Boeselager was born in the Rhineland in 1917. As an army officer during the war he took part in various attempts on Hitler's life, including the famous Stauffenberg plot, 'Operation Valkyrie'. After the war he became a forestry expert and was later honoured by both France and Germany for his bravery. For many years he was the sole survivor of the conspiracy. He died in May 2008.

OPERATION VALKYRIE
The Plot to Kill Hitler

Philipp von Boeselager

with
Florence and Jérôme Fehrenbach

Translated by Steven Rendall

WEIDENFELD & NICOLSON

A W&N PAPERBACK

First published in Great Britain in 2009
by Weidenfeld & Nicolson
This paperback edition published in 2009
by Weidenfeld & Nicolson
an imprint of the Orion Publishing Group
Carmelite House, 50 Victoria Embankment
London EC4Y 0DZ

An Hachette UK company

Reissued 2024

Originally published as *Nous voulions tuer Hitler:
Le dernier survivant du complot du 20 juillet 1944*
Philipp Freiherr von Boeselager © Editions Perrin, 2008
Translation © Weidenfeld & Nicolson, 2009

The right of Philipp von Boeselager to be identified as the
author of this work has been asserted by him in accordance
with the Copyright, Designs and Patents Act 1988.

All rights reserved. No part of this publication may be
reproduced, stored in a retrieval system, or transmitted, in
any form or by any means, electronic, mechanical,
photocopying, recording or otherwise, without the prior
permission of the copyright owner.

A CIP catalogue record for this book
is available from the British Library.

ISBN 978 1 3996 2130 4

Typeset by Input Data Services Ltd, Bridgwater, Somerset

Printed and bound in Great Britain by Clays Ltd, Elcograf, S.p.A.

www.orionbooks.co.uk
www.weidenfeldandnicolson.co.uk

Contents

To my comrades in the Tresckow group,
who made their motto:
Etiam si omnes, ego non!

FOREWORD

Philipp von Boeselager was a rare person. As a member of the conspiracy to kill Hitler, he was a direct witness to perhaps the most important act of German resistance to Nazism of the war. He was also one of the few conspirators to survive until peacetime. After the failed attempt on Hitler's life in July 1944 most of his fellow plotters were rounded up by the SS, tortured and executed. Others, like Philipp's brother Georg, evaded detection only to die fighting against the Allies in the last year of the war. Time eroded their ranks further, and before his own death in 2008, Philipp von Boeselager was the last survivor of this unique group of men. These memoirs are therefore not only a document of his own life and that of his brother, but the final testament of the group as a whole.

Inspired by his disgust at Nazi atrocities on the Eastern Front, Philipp joined the conspiracy at the end of 1942. He was recruited by Henning von Tresckow, the group's leader, and from the very beginning took an active role in planning Hitler's assassination. Over the next eighteen months he was involved in various attempts on Hitler's life, some of which are described in this book, but most of which were ultimately foiled by Hitler's own unpredictable behaviour.

The last of these plots, and the most famous, was the attempt by Claus von Stauffenberg to blow up Hitler at his East Prussian headquarters. Once again, Philipp von Boeselager was intimately involved with this plot, and was charged with acquiring and delivering the explosives that would be used to construct the bomb. He and his brother were then supposed to lead their respective cavalry units to Berlin to take part in the coup that would finally oust the Nazis from power. Had they succeeded it is entirely possible that the war would have ended in 1944, and millions of lives would have been saved.

In retrospect, Stauffenberg was probably the wrong choice for the role of Hitler's assassin. Having been wounded during a bombing raid in North Africa, he had lost an eye, his right hand and two fingers from his left hand – all of which would hamper him during his assassination attempt. And yet his courage and determination are beyond doubt. As this book makes clear, to talk about killing their leader was one thing, but it required a particular kind of bravery and determination to carry out the task in reality. For all his physical handicaps, Stauffenberg was one of the few members of the group who had the moral fortitude to carry the plot through to its conclusion.

The chosen day for the assassination attempt was 20 July 1944. On that day, Stauffenberg arrived at Hitler's headquarters with a briefcase containing two small bombs. On the pretence that he needed to change his shirt, he retired to a nearby room to set the detonators, and this was where his disabilities became a problem.

With only three fingers, setting the fuses proved to be a difficult operation, and he had only succeeded in arming one of the bombs before he was interrupted by a guard opening the door to tell him that the meeting was about to begin. Leaving the second bomb unarmed, Stauffenberg returned to the briefing room, where he placed his briefcase under the table as near to Hitler as possible. Then, pretending that he needed to make an urgent phone call, he left the room and waited in a nearby hut until he heard the explosion.

There has been much speculation in recent years about how Hitler survived the blast. The most common theory is that the explosion was deflected by the heavy oak legs of the table under which the bomb was placed. Had the explosives been put in a different position, or if the second bomb had been armed, it is likely that Hitler would not have survived.

And yet, unbeknown to Stauffenberg, Hitler did indeed survive. Having witnessed the blast, Stauffenberg flew immediately to Berlin to join the rest of the plotters, who by this time were supposed to be staging a coup. It was only when he arrived that he discovered the bad news: the assassination had failed, and the coup had been called off. Within a few hours he was captured, and early the following morning he was executed by firing squad.

The months that followed saw a nationwide purge in which scores of Stauffenberg's fellow conspirators and their families were executed. Philipp and Georg von Boeselager were extremely fortunate to escape detection. On the day of the assassination attempt they had still not reached Berlin, and they were able to turn their cavalry units around and return to the front without arousing too much suspicion. Even so, Philipp was forced to live with the threat of discovery for the rest of the war. That he was never given away by any of the captured conspirators, some of whom were subjected to horrific torture, is a further testament to the bravery of these men.

In the atmosphere of increasing paranoia that characterised the final months of the war, he was obliged to keep his involvement in the plot entirely secret. His isolation was made worse by the death in action of his brother and co-conspirator, Georg, in the late summer of 1944. Certain by this point that Germany was doomed to lose the war, he simply kept his head down, and devoted the next eight months to protecting the lives of his cavalrymen.

As his co-writers Florence and Jérôme Fehrenbach say in their Afterword, secrecy proved a hard habit to break. Even after the war Philipp found it difficult to talk about the conspiracy (and, as Florence Fehrenbach reveals, there were one or two other quite startling secrets that he also managed to keep). His decision to record his memories towards the end of his life came from the realisation that, as the last survivor of the plot, it was his responsibility to bear witness to the bravery of the men he had known.

In January 2004, the French government made Philipp von Boeselager an officer of the Légion d'honneur. He died four years later, on 1 May 2008.

Keith Lowe

A Taste for Freedom

My brother Georg was born in August 1915, I in September 1917, the fourth and fifth children in a family of nine children in total.

My family had settled in Heimerzheim (in the Rhineland) in 1910, leaving our old home in Bonn, which in the eighteenth century had been one of the residences of Prince-Archbishop Clemens-August of Bavaria.[1] With its network of canals and moats, its great central building, white, gabled and flanked by corner towers, it stood on an island reached by a succession of bridges, like a summer palace in ancient China. Its immense grounds were left in a half-wild state where deer peacefully grazed and the familiar mixture of mystery and nature on the doorstep made Heimerzheim seem to us like a fairy-tale castle. There, nothing was easier than to retreat into a secret world. Imagination and children's games could hardly find a more propitious place to develop.

We had a liberal upbringing at Heimerzheim, something that always surprised the guests who passed through – and they were many, since our mother believed that those who had the good fortune to live in a great residence should keep an open house. But for all that, our upbringing was not permissive. Life was very clearly structured, framed by a few strictly defined moral principles: for example, it was forbidden to torture animals. Within this framework, we enjoyed a great deal of leeway.

My father, Albert von Boeselager, was a cultured man of letters. Originally from Brussels on his mother's side, he considered the European nobility a single unit. He hunted all over the continent and spoke four or five languages.

In view of this, he attached particular importance to learning how to make proper use of freedom – and the capacity for Christian discernment which was for him its corollary – and of hunting. Georg received his first rifle as a Christmas present in 1928, when he was barely thirteen years old. At fifteen, my brother's list of kills already included some 150 head of game. His passion was such that he managed to sneak a disassembled rifle into our boarding school – with my complicity, I must admit. When Father Strasser made the rounds of the bedrooms to check the students' bags, we were forced once again to engage in a ruse. Each of us slipped part of the rifle into his pants – Georg the barrel and I the stock – while the inspection took place. The manoeuvre was acrobatic, because it was strictly forbidden to put one's hands in one's pockets, but somehow we had to prevent the parts of the rifle from slipping out.

It was hunting that truly shaped our behaviour in nature. It profoundly influenced our way of life. Georg, in particular, learned to find his way in the forest even before the sun came up, to creep up to within a few metres of a woodcock without putting the bird to flight, to slip through the bushes without making the leaves rustle so as not to frighten the deer, to disappear into the vegetation, perfectly camouflaged, to wait patiently, silent and inactive, in the hide, and to act within a fraction of a second. In a word, hunting, practised in a group or in the course of long solitary hikes, with that passion for animals that marks true nature lovers, made Georg a real Indian. He remained one. This training was to prove extremely valuable.

Hunting was not only a way of hardening the body. It prepared us, without our being aware of it, for the laws of life, for the struggles of existence: preserving one's strength, fleeing from an adversary, recovering, knowing how to use cunning, adapting to the enemy, assessing risk. We learned how to keep our sangfroid in the tumult of dogs excited by the battle, how to strike the throat of a stag or a boar in the coup de grâce and look without revulsion at the dark red fluid bubbling out of mortal wounds. We did not shiver on seeing the brown trickle running down the light-coloured pelt of a young deer, or the bloody foam staining the chops of an animal exhausted by the chase. We withstood the glassy stare of the dead animal and, finally, collected these bloody, damp trophies, the *opima spolies* of modern times. Hunting also accustomed us to the laws of violent death, internalized the notion of an offering. Yes, hunting was a preparation for the supreme sacrifice – the sacrifice of life.

The education we received at Godesberg did not differ from what we were taught at Heimerzheim, which I would call 'relaxed Catholicism'. My family was profoundly Catholic, with a centuries-old history linked to that of the German Catholic princes. In the seventeenth century, our ancestors the Heyden-Belderbusches, from whom we had inherited the Heimerzheim castle, were ministers of the powerful archbishop of Cologne. During the same period, the Satzenhovens, from whom we had inherited the Kreuzberg estate, were in the service of the prince-electors of Mainz.

As children, Georg and I were very close. Separated by only two years, we were like Castor and Pollux – natural playmates, and accomplices in the same practical jokes. But this intimacy, which made us almost a separate unit among our siblings, did not prevent us from developing different qualities, nor did it diminish the natural ascendancy of the elder child over the younger. As a duo, our strength was based on our complementing one another. Georg was physically more robust, more athletic, more intuitive, and had an instinctive perceptiveness regarding people, situations and things. I, on the other hand, was more reflective and analytical. Two anecdotes from our early childhood clearly show, I think, our difference in character.

At Heimerzheim, the grounds were full of wild deer. The animals sometimes came quite close to the house. One day, our older brothers Antonius and Hermann, who were then not quite ten, were amusing themselves by trying to provoke one of the deer by throwing pebbles at it. Sitting behind a stone bench, Georg was watching carefully. The roebuck, suddenly responding to the little devils' challenge, decided to attack. Georg reacted with lightning swiftness; all of five years old, he seized the rifle that Antonius had left leaning against the bench and shot at the animal. Ka-boom! Bowled over by the rifle's recoil, Georg fell backwards. Fortunately, he was not hurt. But the explosion had frightened away the roebuck.

As for me, when I was four years old I distinguished myself at a family dinner. Our cousin zu Stolberg-Stolberg had been seriously wounded in the head during the Great War. The surgeons had installed a silver plate on his skull to close the hole left by enemy fire, and he lived a long time after being wounded, not dying until the 1960s. I had heard about this extraordinary operation and wanted to see the result for myself. Climbing silently onto a chair, I leaned over my cousin's head and began to examine, discreetly and carefully, the bald area where the precious metal shone. They say that I then cried, disappointed, 'That's not silver! There's no hallmark!' As a reward for this pertinent observation, I received a couple of slaps ...

To tell the truth, our father never took much interest in his children's scholastic achievements. After several years of taking lessons at home, however, the boys had to be subjected to modern education. 'School,' our father said, sighing, 'is an obligation these days. It's very boring, but you've got to do it!' So we were enrolled in the Aloïsius Jesuit secondary school in Godesberg, in the outskirts of Bonn. As it turned out, entering boarding school was not very traumatic. Heimerzheim was at that time less than an hour's drive by car from the school. The Jesuit teaching provided at Aloïsius did not seek to train priests, but to reconcile the sacred and the profane in human beings, and to keep alive the flame of faith amid the chaos of the world. Practising religion was not supposed to be an end in itself; it was supposed to slip naturally into the schedules, the lives, and, as it were, the skins of the young boys. The five or six years we spent in Godesberg helped root in us a solid, authentic, uncomplicated, moderate faith. Ultimately, we were taught more a way of behaving than a body of knowledge, although nothing was omitted from the regular curriculum. In any case, we learned the most important thing that can be learned in school: how to learn.

The headmaster of the boarding school was a patriot. As he saw it, Christian values, humanism, the sense of honour, respect for others, the tradition of intellectual rigour and critical vigilance that had long characterized Jesuit pedagogy were not incompatible with love of country. It is revealing that none of my classmates later became a Nazi supporter. This fact, which was rather exceptional in my generation, deserves to be noted.

THE TIME OF CHOICES
(1933–1936)

In 1933, when the Nazis came to power, Georg was not yet eighteen years old; I was barely fifteen. Thus at the time, this event, although later it turned out to be crucial for us and our families, left us rather indifferent. Our parents, though they certainly did not adhere to the ideology of the Nazi party, were not sorry to see the end of the Weimar Republic.

We knew what it was to feel humiliated after a defeat. Because we lived on the left bank of the Rhine, which was under Allied occupation, between 1919 and 1926 we saw Canadian, British and then French troops – chiefly drawn from the colonies – march past. These six years of peacetime occupation were long and burdensome. For Germans, the situation was incomprehensible: enemy troops had not entered the country on the western frontier, there had been no invasion during the war, and now it was the peace treaty, a treaty considered unjust and designed to ruin the country, that brought about foreign occupation. A period of occupation, even a tranquil one, is hardly likely to strengthen friendship among peoples. The occupation of the Ruhr from 1923 to 1926 was accompanied by violence and turmoil, and resulted in 121 summary executions and tens of thousands of expulsions, and it led to a general strike – at the instigation of Chancellor Cuno – and the economic collapse of the industrial heart of Germany, bringing on terrifying inflation. All that, I think, accentuated the Rhinelanders' already very strong prejudice against the French, who had been seen for centuries as troublesome neighbours. The humiliations inflicted by the occupying forces did not escape my notice when I was a child. I remember that my parents had been forbidden to attend the burial of my grandmother, on the pretext that my father was a reserve officer. I also recall how we congratulated Father Seelen, who had dared to sing the German national anthem, which was strictly prohibited on the left bank, in full view of the French troops. Fortunately Father Seelen was a Dutch citizen, and the French could not arrest him. That is how, as young men, we practised a kind of resistance that was within our capabilities.

My father believed in European unity before it became fashionable to do so; he was not at all inclined to be vindictive. But as a former officer in the Great War, he was a patriot and he wanted to see Germany regain all its rights as a great nation. He communicated this desire to us without imposing it on us. And our elder brother Antonius quite naturally joined the paramilitary Stahlhelm.

I could understand it if a foreign reader felt a certain mistrust regarding the political position of German patriots of that period, and was tempted to see in it an inadmissible compromise with the goals pursued by Hitler. We were nonetheless able to tell the difference. We had no more need to be ashamed of wanting to restore Germany than had the French who in 1914 wanted to return Alsace and Lorraine to France.

I must describe something that happened to me at that time which taught me a little about the methods used by Hitler's men. In 1934 the chancellor of the Reich came to Bonn. Curious, I climbed over my boarding school's wall, accompanied by a classmate. We approached the Dreesen Hotel, where the chancellor was supposed to be staying, and found a hiding place where we might at least catch a glimpse of him on the steps. We were found out. Two SS-men picked us up, and without further investigation simply locked us up in a garage. We were terrified that the headmaster of the school, informed of our escape, might punish us. Our internment, without food and without sleep, lasted until the early hours of the morning, but once the chancellor had departed, we were set free. Miraculously, our desertion had not been noticed at the school. I would like to say that during that day and the following night we had plenty to think about.

The somewhat suspicious nature of the Nazi movement was soon revealed in another way. The headmaster of the school in Bad-Godesberg, Father Rodewyck, a Jesuit and a former military officer in the Great War, was not indifferent to the revival of patriotism. But he was able to channel the ardour of the boys entrusted to him, providing a Christian framework within his school and avoiding any pollution by Nazi ideology. Thus in 1933 Georg founded a Catholic patriotic movement in the school whose scouting spirit was indicated by its attachment to moral and religious values. It was called the

Jungstahlheim. Along similar lines, the Jesuit school founded a movement on the model of Hitler's *Deutsche Jungvolk* or 'Pimpfen', whose activities (camping, hiking, etc.) then seemed quite innocent. Father Rodewyck had seen the risk that hearts and souls might be won by the Nazi party's youth organizations, and he preferred to infiltrate the movement using boys like us. Our headmaster thought he had done what was necessary to keep control of the organization. But it gradually escaped the grasp of the school and its headmaster.

It was at this time that another important episode occurred. I belonged to a club devoted to Our Lady, the Congregation of Mary. One fine day in the summer of 1937, the head of my group of Pimpfen, a nice fellow, came to tell me that belonging to the valiant Pimpfen was incompatible with religiosity, and so I had to choose between the two. I was intelligent; he was sure that he would succeed in persuading me to give up my membership in the Congregation of Mary without hesitation. But I flatly refused. I found it intolerable to be forced to make such a choice and did not hesitate. I have to admit that I did not reveal the precise motive for my refusal. I told him only that preparing for my final school examination prevented me from continuing to participate in these activities. The pretext seemed valid, and it was accepted.

Georg took his final exam in the summer of 1934. He had already made a decision regarding his future: he wanted to be a military officer. My brother had a taste for action and initiative. He excelled in all athletic disciplines, had inexhaustible energy, and showed great endurance. He liked the outdoor life. And in the end, he was interested in human psychology. Objectively, everything pointed him toward this profession. At that time people believed, not without a certain *naïveté*, that entering the army was also a way of serving one's country without serving the government. It seemed to us that the army was the only institution that had remained faithful to its principles and was capable, through its vitality and culture, of preserving its identity and, especially, its autonomy with respect to the government. In 1934, for a young man like Georg, a military career still seemed to make it possible to reconcile a taste for action with independence.

Georg then had to choose his branch. He opted for the cavalry. He was built like a jockey and was almost as thin. When he asked to be admitted to the regiment, I remember that he was told that he was not heavy enough. My father wrote to the commandant and appealed to the ministry. Finally, the military administration agreed that, except on this one point, Georg had all the required physical aptitudes. They were not wrong. During his years of training in military schools and then in the Paderborn 15th Cavalry Regiment, Georg spent a great deal of time perfecting his equestrian technique, and much of his leisure time competing in races. By 1939 he had participated in about a hundred competitions.

In 1936, I was confronted by the same choice. I had a somewhat romantic view of a diplomatic career, which attracted me. To that end, I had even begun learning Arabic. I could already write the alphabet and read a little. Shortly after taking my examination, I went to ask the advice of my maternal grandfather, Baron von Salis-Soglio. He was a liberal man with firm convictions. In his youth, he had distinguished himself by resigning his post as a governmental official in protest against a disciplinary transfer to East Prussia, which he had received as punishment for participating in a Corpus Christi procession. To do this in that part of Germany, which was historically Catholic and had been joined to Protestant Prussia after the treaties of Vienna, was proof of a strong spirit of independence. We had full confidence in the sureness of his judgements. My grandfather told me straight out, 'My boy, in diplomacy, it's not always good to tell the whole truth; but with Nazis, you'd have to simply lie. No, that wouldn't be suitable for you! Choose the army instead; war is coming.'

This advice was typical of my grandfather's lucidity: Germany had just rearmed, despite the provisions of the Versailles Treaty, and in March 1936 it had remilitarized the right bank of the Rhine: gunpowder was in the air. It was judicious to learn the soldier's trade. So after having completed my classes in Döberitz during the summer of 1938 I joined my brother in the Paderborn cavalry regiment. At first, I was in the reserves. Then, following Georg's example, I began training to be an active officer.

In the meantime, I had done my compulsory work service in Merseburg. My group was made up of fifteen Rhinelanders and the same number of Bavarians, and the two contingents were unable to speak with one another because each knew only its own dialect. We were supposed to help construct a dike. I was an engine driver and my job was to bring construction materials to the site. The atmosphere wasn't bad; we had agreed not to compete with each other – the Bavarians conscientiously soaped the rails before dawn so that the materials would arrive more slowly. Everybody benefited. But it was a Spartan life. We slept on pallets on the concrete floor of a shed. The people in charge were not intelligent. The indoctrination sessions were so mediocre that they ended a quarter of an hour early in a gale of laughter. I was careful not to judge this experience negatively; this obligation was an additional proof of the absurdity of certain of the regime's measures, but after all, I had taken advantage of it to harden myself a little, and I got along well with my fellow Rhinelanders.

It would be an exaggeration to say that our vigilance with regard to the regime had already been awakened at that point. The officers were trained in a completely apolitical way, as if the Wehrmacht, the heir of the Reichswehr, an eternal institution, were situated sufficiently above the vicissitudes of the time to be indifferent to them. We were entirely devoted to our military training and, since we lived in barracks far from the cities and were cut off from the press, we were not well informed. I have to admit that the famous encyclical *Mit brennender Sorge* ('With Burning Anxiety'), which denounced Nazism, had hardly any effect on me. I was barely twenty years old; at that age, one easily forgets encyclicals read from the pulpit, and one certainly does not read them for amusement!

However, one important point attracted my attention. For a time after Hitler's accession to power, my father had a Nazi party card. This was not because he was a supporter out of personal conviction, or even because it was opportune. He had allowed himself to be persuaded by people from the village who had come in 1934 to ask him to join the party. Our father was one of the main figures in the nobility of the Rhineland. I think he saw the question in the following terms, as did many other people of his social group: did he have the right, on the pretext of belonging to the aristocracy, to disdain this vast movement of national renewal? Did he have the privilege of not joining in this groundswell that was carrying millions of Germans in its wake? Did he, whom the local population considered a true gentleman, have good reasons for preserving a distant attitude that might look like arrogance or folly, or even scorn for the popular elements that constituted most of the movement's membership?

However that may be, our father quickly returned to his feelings of reservation and even outright hostility concerning the regime. In 1937, the government, which was violating with increasing frequency the concordat signed with the Holy See in July 1933, decided to remove crucifixes from the schools. This attack, even if only symbolic, on Germany's Christian identity seemed to him inadmissible. Since 1919, the Weimar Republic had been trying to find, region by region, a delicate balance in the relations between Church and state.[2] More generally, the Church's discreet influence persisted at all levels of the education of young people. The Nazis' sabotage was going to destroy all these achievements. This said a great deal about the regime's totalitarian aims. Therefore our father resigned from the party in 1938, at a time when the annexation of Austria was leading many people to join it. The Nazis responded by forcing him to resign from organizations of which he was the president, notably the National League for the Defence of Hunting.

Another ground for concern, and even for consternation, was the regime's anti-Jewish policy. From legal restrictions, which had rapidly become so numerous that it was difficult to tell which ones were marginal and which were essential, it moved on to physical persecution, and finally to routine violence. There were three Jewish families in our little town of Heimerzheim. Our father, aware of the danger, advised them to go rapidly into exile. He even offered to pay their travel costs. Two families followed his advice and emigrated to the United States. The father in the third family, whose name was Moses, did not do so. He thought the Iron Cross he had been awarded for his service in the trenches in 1914 would ensure that he would be left alone. He was badly mistaken. A few years later, he was arrested along with the rest of his family. We never saw them again.

Even if the information at our disposal in the barracks was limited, Kristallnacht in November 1938 did not escape our attention. I remember perfectly that it was talked about quite freely among officers and students. In the local newspaper, we read only that 'Three shops were ransacked in Western Street'. At first, we did not realize that this was part of a more general phenomenon that had affected all of Germany. Further information dribbled in over the next few days, especially through correspondence between our men and their families in different parts of the country. For us, public order was non-negotiable, and a pogrom was an unprecedented violation of rights and public peace that was inadmissible in a civilized country. We all agreed – perhaps with a certain ingenuousness – that if we had been present in town when exactions were made we would have made use of the dispositions of the criminal code regarding legitimate defence, which we knew by heart. Our commandant assured us that the courts would take action. Later on, when we realized the full measure of the atrocities committed, we were for a time persuaded that the generals would act. For us, it was unthinkable that the law could be violated with impunity in Germany, without anyone doing anything about it. But nothing was done, apart from our commandant's assurances and consolations.

That said, the cavalry regiment was hermetically sealed off from much of the outside world. Constructing a spirit of comradeship was for us more important than pretending to be citizens of the world. Sports were far more important than political discussion. Jumping and dressage were our daily occupations. I had fewer physical abilities than Georg, and had to catch up. To lose weight and not to receive humiliating scores on the racecourse, I even had to fast from Tuesday to Saturday. A hard school! But a good school, for my captain was Rudolph Lippert, the Olympic equestrian champion at the 1936 games.

The days were long and the training athletic and motivating. Each morning, summer and winter, we left on our motorcycles at dawn, heading for Quelle, 48 kilometres away near Bielefeld, where there was a fine racecourse. The regiment kept race-horses there, which were made available to officers in order to improve their skills. The horses were waiting for us, already saddled up. We leapt into the saddle, made two or three circuits around the course, handed the reins to a groom, hopped on our motorcycles, and hurried to take showers when we arrived back at the school. Our orderlies were waiting for us with towels and fresh clothes. Then we went, more or less in good spirits, to the morning roll call and by 7.30 we were ready to begin the work day proper, which included several additional hours of equestrian exercises.

THE PHONEY WAR
(1939–1940)

When war broke out on 1 September 1939, the Paderborn cavalry regiment – which was for us almost a second family – was dissolved, like the thirteen other groups of mounted cavalry in the Wehrmacht before mobilization. We were divided up into 52 squadrons scattered over 33 infantry divisions. We were supposed to be integrated into reconnaissance battalions whose mission was – by reconnoitring, establishing bridgeheads, and in short all kinds of bold actions – to prepare the way for the less mobile groups of heavy infantry. The reconnaissance battalions, each consisting of about a thousand men, included a staff with its support functions (administration, food supplies, intelligence...), a cavalry squadron, a cycle squadron and a heavy motorized squadron. They had excellent communications equipment, especially radios.

The first months of the war passed rather peacefully. Georg and I were assigned to the area along the borders with Luxembourg and France, Georg in the 6th Infantry division, and I in the 86th. Georg became head of the 6th Cavalry Squadron, with our elder brother Tonio, who was a reservist, under his command. Tonio in turn headed a detachment of about fifty cavalrymen. To tell the truth, this 'phoney war' was not without fighting, even on a front that was said to be quiet. On 8 September, no less than six divisions of the French Fourth Army advanced several kilometres into German territory, between Forbach and Bitche, and were about to enter into contact with the Siegfried Line, which was situated at some distance from the border. Georg's unit was involved in a few skirmishes with the French troops. As for myself, I was assigned to retake a French position, in the middle of the night. The enemy's disarray was complete, because they hadn't anticipated that we would approach it by the most difficult side. The French withdrew from our sector in October.

This period of semi-inaction allowed the officers to complete the training of the reservists who had been mobilized during the summer and – a temptation not to be resisted when autumn came – to hunt in the game-filled forests along the banks of the Moselle.

A Dive for Victory
(9 June 1940)

Incorporated into the Fourth Army in Army Group B, the 6th Infantry Division entered France on 16 May, a few days after the large armoured and motorized groups that had overwhelmed the French defences. By 28 May, it had reached the Somme and was beginning to tack towards the south-west. The army group caught Paris in a sling on the north and west, while Army Group, crossing the Aisne, threatened the capital's eastern flank and then headed for Burgundy.

On 9 June, the 6th Division forced its way across the Seine and set up bridgeheads around Les Andelys.[3] At noon, the French blew up the bridge at Les Andelys, which a German advance unit had tried to seize. For the Germans, the day had begun in a confused way and seemed not very promising. The 6th Reconnaissance Battalion moved a few kilometres up the Seine, but toward 3 p.m. the French blew up the bridge at Courcelles.

It was then that Georg's sense of initiative came fully to the fore. He had noticed an organizational weakness in the French defence. Opposite the hamlet of Les Mousseaux, there were only a few isolated soldiers, and they lacked heavy artillery. At that place, the river narrowed slightly, and was only about 180 metres across. The banks of the river were muddy, spongy, unstable and covered with tall grass, reeds and even brambles – no place to go swimming! But Georg quickly made a decision. It was pointless to wait for inflatable boats; precious minutes would be lost. He selected a squad of good swimmers. Led by my brother, twelve men rapidly undressed and moved into the river, armed with a few rifles and hand grenades. The rest of the squad was assigned to provide artillery cover for their attack. Three of these men drowned almost at once, probably as a result of the shock of the cold water and exhaustion after almost four weeks of constant activity. In addition, for the past two days, the squadron had been without food supplies.

The French were taken completely by surprise. They could not have anticipated being attacked by a simple squad of cavalry that had made itself amphibious. Georg's little squad had caught its breath on a tiny island in the middle of the river. A few French snipers were hidden in the vegetation on the opposite bank, but the fire from a German machine gun set up on the right bank quickly dislodged them from their hiding place. The left bank of the Seine was now undefended. Georg and his men rapidly occupied it and climbed a few metres up the embankment. They had to stop when they reached the edge. The village of Grand-Villiers which lay in front of them had a few defenders. It would have been madness to operate in the open. The alert had no doubt been sounded, and French reinforcements would be on their way. But the little group had established a bridgehead. Inflatable boats were now bringing men and materiel from the other side of the river. In a few minutes, sixty men and some light artillery had been unloaded on the left bank. An hour later, the whole cavalry squadron, both men and horses, had passed over.

Shortly afterwards, a detachment led by our brother Tonio took Grand-Villiers. Georg and his men stopped a French motorized column dead in its tracks as it advanced along the road to Les Andelys. Twenty minutes later, they intercepted an artillery column. During the fifteen hours that followed, the French made four attempts to retake Grand-Villiers. In vain.

Even if on 9 June the victory was already won, Georg's action nonetheless entered the Wehrmacht's annals as an exploit, and made my brother famous for a few days. It was, in a way, another version of the seizure of Sedan on 10 May. Crossing the Seine made it possible to attack Paris from the opposite side and to deprive our enemies of any hopes of turning the military situation around – if they still entertained such hopes.

On 16 June, Georg and his men distinguished them-selves once again. The scene took place at Marchainville, near the castle of Persay. The French were defending themselves well. An artillery battalion prevented the Germans from advancing. Georg and his squad managed to get around the obstacle. They abruptly attacked from the rear. There were no casualties on either side; the French immediately surrendered. The booty was invalu-able: three 75 millimetre guns, gun carriages, and ... the prospect of a good dinner. To the amazement of the French, Georg collected all the provisions and canned goods, and said 'fifty-fifty' with an eloquent gesture. The French and the Germans thus ate their meals side by side. They almost managed to make friends during this improvised picnic. But then my brother suddenly noticed several French tanks approaching: the power relationship had been reversed. It was no longer time for joking. In a few seconds, Georg and his men packed up, left their table-mates and the food, and got out of the clearing as fast as they could. My brother's military technique and behaviour inclined him to save lives and avoid unnecessary fighting.

A Promise
(17 June 1940)

While Georg was leading his men through the Paris basin, I was serving as an aide-de-camp to the commandant of the 186th Reconnaissance Battalion – within the 86th Infantry Division of Army Group A. We had started out from Hermeskeil, near Trier, traversed Luxemburg, and entered France by way of Sedan. After hard fighting near Rethel, we were getting ready to move onto the Langres plateau, making a wide sweep towards the Swiss border.[4]

On 17 June, my battalion was stationed in Allianville, near Grand. In the commandant's absence, I was temporarily in charge. We were supposed to attack the town of Prez, a few kilometres to the south, when a certain incident prevented us from doing so. The head of a heavy artillery battery, a man named Auer who was very concerned about his own comfort, had brought along his personal car, and this was equipped with a radio (something that was unusual at the time). The afternoon was well advanced when he came to tell me what he had just heard: the French news programme had announced that Marshal Pétain was preparing to ask Germany for an armistice. I mentioned this to Rudolf von Gersdorff, the head of the operations section of the Division's staff.

The news was not official; there was neither a confirmed ceasefire nor any formal order in this regard. But we believed that the information was crucial and justified us in changing our conduct. It seemed clear to us that it would be useless and even criminal to shed any more blood at this stage. Therefore on our own initiative – and this was certainly not usual for officers of a victorious army – we decided to establish contact with the enemy.

We found out which points of the road had been mined from a French colonel who had been taken prisoner. After attaching a white flag to a broomstick, we requisitioned a bugle and a car, and in this noble equipage Gersdorff and I approached the French lines. A sentry came to enquire what we wanted. The officer in charge of the French battalion was sought out. He was a mere lieutenant; like me, he was standing in for the leader of the battalion, who had left the day before to get instructions. The French lieutenant, after having had us blindfolded, took us to the battalion's command post. It was 5 p.m. The Frenchman knew nothing about the request for a ceasefire and stated that he had been instructed to hold his position until precisely 7 p.m. Afterwards, he was supposed to withdraw. As gentlemen, we thus agreed that the Germans would start moving after 7 p.m, and would occupy the village only after the last French troops had left it.

Satisfied with this arrangement, we returned to Aillianville. Gersdorff asked me to see to the execution of the terms of the agreement, and went back to the divisional headquarters, which he had left several hours earlier and to which he said he absolutely must return.

A few moments later, Lieutenant-Colonel Doege came up to me. The infantry regiment he commanded was moving south, and he coldly informed me of his intention to attack Prez.

'Impossible, Colonel,' I replied. 'We have an agreement with the French. They've asked for a ceasefire.' I explained the situation. The lieutenant-colonel did not want to hear about it, either because he wanted to distinguish himself by some new feat, or because he did not have much confidence in what I said.

'Sorry to displease you,' he said, 'but I'm going to give the order to attack.'

I could see that the colonel was determined, and that his foolishness was probably going to cost the lives of dozens of men in both camps, so I decided to pull out all the stops. As calmly as possible, and fully aware of the disciplinary consequences that might result from what I was about to do, I drew my pistol and pointed it at the colonel.

'It is I who am sorry, but if you give this order I will have to shoot you,' I said, very carefully.

The lieutenant colonel exploded with anger. But seeing the pistol pointed at him and seeing that I looked serious – what a good actor I was – he yielded. The French battalion was saved. Everything went as planned, without shedding a drop of blood. Few people knew what had happened, and we tried to keep it quiet. But we were unable to keep the news from circulating among the staffs. The story became almost a legend – in some versions, I actually fired. Fortunately, as the anecdote spread and became garbled, the names of the two people involved were forgotten. In any case, until the end of the war Doege and I took care to avoid each other . . .

A Lightning Campaign
(June–November 1941)

The end of the campaign in France inaugurated a period of almost nine months of peace. We took advantage of this time of relative calm to train men and horses, and especially to hunt. Fate had been good to me: I was based south of Orléans, in the middle of Sologne, a hunter's paradise. There I lived in a house deserted by wealthy Parisians who had fled to the South. I still have very pleasant memories of those few months when the German occupation was, obviously, still not too painful for the French, or at least did not yet elicit hostile reactions.

My brother Georg was less fortunate. During the summer his squadron was located in Chaunay, on the road from Poitiers to Angoulême. Chaunay was already almost in the South, in that part of Vienne that is close to Charente. The sparsely wooded countryside, rather poorly maintained, was hardly suitable for hunting, and poachers seemed already to have skimmed off the area's limited amount of game: neither big game, nor tracking, nor even battues; no wild ducks or partridges. Cats (which Georg abhorred), dogs and sparrows were the only wild animals. No matter! On 23 July, a few days after they had established themselves in Chaunay, Georg organized his first hunt, and invited the head of the battalion.

Georg's superior was cantoned some 15 kilometres away, and the division was scattered over the whole department of Vienne. Lodged in a mansion that looked out on the main square, my brother reigned over his village and commanded his 250 men as he wished. They were, however, not entirely idle; during the summer, his squadron had to deal with the flow of tens of thousands of French people who had headed south with the exodus, and were now slowly moving north again along national highway 10. The long line of vehicles loaded with mattresses, bicycles, cooking utensils and packages of various kinds stretched as far as one could see, and the heat was pitiless – as high as 50°C in the sun. In addition, Georg and his men had to cope with the angry explosions of an exasperated population. But it was not yet time for revolt. The French still didn't feel that sensation of being crushed which led them to realize that they had been completely and lastingly defeated. They did not yet bend under the weight of the foreign occupation. The infernal cycle of acts of resistance and repressions, and especially that of persecutions and deportations, had not yet begun. A feeling of indifference was dominant. One had to get along, and customs inspired by mutual tolerance were quickly established.[5]

Georg's stay in Vienne was soon over. His division was called upon to participate in the ultra-secret preparations for the invasion of England. In September 1940, it started moving towards the Channel. They took up their position within the Cotentin, the Calvados and the

Orne. Georg was very active in training his men.

But it was not towards England that the 6th Infantry Division was finally to direct its forces. Despite intense bombardments and peace offers followed by threats, Britain, isolated and bled dry, did not falter. Above all, it did not give up the hope of victory. So in March 1941, the 6th Infantry Division was transferred to the far reaches of East Prussia and Poland, very near the line of demarcation with the USSR. No information regarding the staff's intentions filtered down. However, even the less lucid among us noticed the growing concentration of troops, the acceleration of training, and the energy expended by the battalion's new commandant, Major Hirsch, on exploring the border area. All this was merely the prelude to an invasion of the Soviet Union. The 6th Infantry Division was ordered to attack in the early hours of 23 June 1941. The 86th Infantry Division, in which I was an officer, was brought in from France only a few weeks later. We were thus less exposed to the first clashes with the enemy.

At the beginning of a battle, the role of a recon-naissance battalion was crucial. Reconnoitring the terrain, making raids to take prisoners or equipment (munitions and maps), harassing the enemy to demor-alize him without investing great human resources, dis-lodging hidden snipers, making sure that columns advancing at very different speeds joined up where they were supposed to: such were, in their diversity, the scouts' missions. On 18 May, in preparation for the offensive, the command of the Ninth Army decided to split the elite unit constituted by the 6th Reconnaissance

Battalion into two parts. The first, called the advance battalion, still under Hirsch's orders, was placed directly under the command of the Sixth Army. Georg, who was about to be promoted to the rank of captain, was given the leadership of a reconnaissance battalion that consisted only of a cavalry squadron and a cycle squadron, reinforced by an intelligence detachment, and especially by a mortar battery, a heavy machine gun and an anti-aircraft battery. It played a very active role in the first hours of the offensive. By the evening of 22 June, Georg's forces had reached their objective. They were asked to establish a bridgehead on the Memel. After crossing 10 kilometres of marshes and forests, Georg encountered stiff resistance from the enemy. On 25 June, the reconnaissance forces were joined together again, but during this short interval the mounted cavalry, used for the first time in a relatively isolated manner, had shown its flexibility in all sorts of situations.

Around the middle of July, it was again the reconnaissance work carried out by Georg's men that allowed the 6th Division to take, almost without losses, the citadel of Polozk on the Dvina. On 27 July, hardly a month after the beginning of the offensive, the 6th Battalion had covered a thousand kilometres by forced march. The exhausted infantrymen's feet were bleeding, despite the efforts of the doctors, who distributed large quantities of talcum and ointment. The vehicles were dented and covered with dust; logs were being used as bumpers. They advanced laboriously on rutted dirt roads, and sank up to their axles on sandy tracks. Their carburettors scraped the ground, their engines coughed, sputtered, spat out oil and left a trail of nuts and bolts. And when, by some miracle, the convoys were able to get up some speed on solid roads, each vehicle raised a long cloud of dust that spread over a hundred metres, enveloping those behind it. The horses moved forward almost imperturbably, caring little for the marshes or the dust so long as the cavalry detachments were separated from each other by at least a hundred metres. They went briskly around obstacles, plunged up to their breasts in the sticky water of the marshes, galloped ... and always arrived at the rendezvous on time. But the cavalry couldn't advance alone. It was mobile, but not invulnerable. The strikes it attempted resulted in casualties every time its troops were not properly covered by the artillery.

Until late July, the advance of the units to which Georg and I belonged was extremely rapid. We were on the road to Moscow, taking more or less Napoleon's route. The enemy's resistance was weak and his morale was failing. In view of the collapse of the Russian Army, which was moreover practising scorched-earth tactics, opinion in the country was on the whole very favourable to us.[6] So we were optimistic about the outcome of the operations. We thought Russia's fate would be decided within six weeks. But Russia wasn't France. A Blitzkrieg was impossible in a country of several tens of millions of square kilometres. At the end of July, our advance halted. On this terrain, the enemy had recovered. The threat to Moscow was too direct not to elicit a response, and the 6th Infantry Division had to adopt a defensive position around Borki on the Mesha.

The month of August was difficult. There were daily skirmishes with the enemy. Placed under the authority of the 58th Infantry Regiment, Georg's unit was being used for reconnaissance missions on the left flank, which the Russians had penetrated by crossing the Dvina. On 1 August, the cavalry repelled an enemy battalion that outnumbered them four to one back onto the far bank of the river. On 2 August, the reconnaissance battalion found itself surrounded after a co-ordinated attack by two Russian cavalry divisions. My brother's squadron was quickly brought back to the battalion to which it was attached. There was no time to lose. Although it was already getting dark (it was 7 p.m.), Georg surprised the attacking forces by striking their south flank, between Agejeva and Shichova. Supported by artillery, he inflicted severe losses on the adversary. The fighting went on all that night and the following day. The day after that, the Russian attack was over, and the connection between the division and its reconnaissance battalion was restored.

However, these missions soon took a tragic turn. On the evening of 4 August, Tonio, who had been put under Georg's direct command in one of the skirmishes in which the squadron was regularly engaged, was hit by a bullet and fell from his mount. He remained on the battlefield while Georg and his cavalrymen, carried forward by their momentum, pursued the scattered Russians. The medics ran to help Tonio and discovered that he had a wound in his abdomen – a serious one, according to a preliminary diagnosis carried out in the twilight, but not mortal. His intestines and spleen had been damaged.

He was taken to the field hospital but died the next day from an embolism, after an operation that seemed to have gone well. He was buried in a nearby cemetery, near an old church that the Soviets had converted into a wheat barn. Georg and I were shattered. Fortunately, we were able to see each other on 26 and 27 August, because my division was in a neighbouring sector. These moments spent together provided us with a little consolation and a way to share our suffering as brothers. This was, alas, not the only sacrifice that that year was to impose on us, because on 30 November we lost our youngest brother as well.

In early October, we began offensive operations again. Georg's division moved forward into a marshy area that was impractical for motorized vehicles. The autumn, which was too warm, hampered the armies' advance: the freeze was late in coming. It rained constantly, obstinately. The roads turned into sewers. Trucks, bogged down in the mud, ran out of fuel, and food supplies could not get through. At times Georg and his horses were almost a hundred kilometres ahead of the rest of their division. The month of October practically decided the fate of the war. It was soon clear that we could not take Moscow before December, when the terrible Russian winter would set in. The officers thought about the ill-fated French episode in 1812. The autumn had stalled our forward momentum and winter would prevent any further advance.

In any case, the 6th Infantry succeeded in fulfilling its assignment. At the end of October, it descended the Volga, passed to the north of the capital, and reached

Kalinin (now the city of Tver). Georg and his men crossed over to the right bank of the Volga in a sector infested with enemies. They pushed as far as the Tma, one of the great river's tributaries. In a few hours, without losing a single man or being observed, they explored dozens of square kilometres, wrote reports, and sent to their headquarters all the information that might be useful for a prospective penetration. By 15 November, they had an impressive record in the field: they had covered more than 1,300 kilometres, and taken prizes that were considerable for a unit of 200 men: 700 prisoners, 175 horses, 60 horse-drawn vehicles, 10 trucks, and one tank! This record was transmitted, with get-well wishes, to all the squadron's wounded, who were scattered in various military hospitals.

The campaign had been just as brilliant for the division to which I belonged. As far as Smolensk, our losses had been minimal. The fighting around Smolensk lasted from 10 July to 10 September. About 300,000 Soviet troops and 3,000 tanks were surrounded; the Soviets were not about to get themselves killed for Stalin. We gave them back their churches, which had been closed or transformed into storage buildings years earlier. The sinister commissar-order, which called for the execution of Soviet political commissars who had been taken prisoner, never reached my unit and was not applied in my area: under these conditions, whole battalions of Russians were surrendering without a fight. One day, I sent Second Lieutenant von Nagel on patrol a little to the east of Vilnius, and he came back in the evening with about 2,000 prisoners. They were still fully equipped, because the fifteen men in von Nagel's detachment were not numerous enough to disarm them. His men were riding alongside the prisoners like shepherds amid a peaceful flock. It was an incredible sight, unparalleled so far as I know in recent military history.

A few weeks after the fighting ended around Smolensk, the general in command of the division ordered me to scout out the possibilities for crossing the Volga at a ford. Because of the mud, horse-drawn vehicles could not be used and all the motor vehicles had prudently been taken back to the main road to Moscow. Only horsemen could reconnoitre the area ahead. We started out toward Kalinin with provisions for a few days. Using a compass, and guided by the information provided by scouts, we rode for four or five hours and then stopped in a village to bake bread in a farm, surrounded by Russians, because the field canteen had remained with the vehicles. The days went by without any contact with our division. It was as if we had suddenly been transported to the age of the Thirty Years' War. Our squadron encountered neither Russian nor German soldiers. When we arrived in Kalinin, the Volga was completely frozen over, and our search for a ford was no longer relevant. Moreover, armoured divisions had just taken up positions nearby.

Three days later, the division's chaplains arrived in Kalinin. Like the missionaries in the time of Saint Boniface and Saint Patrick, they had crossed the deserted expanse of the Russian plain without encountering a living soul. They hadn't eaten for several days. We immediately gave them some bread baked in the hearth of a peasant home.

Then we went to find quarters in a village south-west of Kalinin. We first tried to gather a supply of oats for the winter, a share of which was taken from each of the surrounding villages. I made the acquaintance of a man who had been a gamekeeper under the Czars, and who had also participated in a hunt organized by Marshal Voroshilov himself, some years earlier. On many occasions we went hunting together on a sleigh, wrapped in the same fur blanket, through the vast zone of marshland and peat bogs south-east of the village. Lulled by the peaceful rhythm of this new life in a frozen countryside, somewhat enervated by long sessions in the sauna and by long card parties around the gigantic earthenware stoves that formed the centre of the Russian cottages, we allowed ourselves to be overcome by the conviction that the war would soon be over. When in early December I saw my gamekeeper for what turned out to be the last time, he greeted me and said: 'I'll see you tomorrow, we're going for our little ducks! Agreed?' So convinced were we that the war was over and that we had no reason to be concerned about our new life. Our awakening was brutal.

A CHRISTMAS IN HELL
(DECEMBER 1941–JANUARY 1942)

On 20 November 1941, Major Hirsch, who had been
assigned to another command, left the 6th Reconnaissance Battalion and my brother succeeded him as
commandant. Projects were arranged to make intelligent
use of the winter. Georg thought of giving Latin courses
and undertook to procure grammar books and dict-
ionaries, and the staff launched a literary competition
and a cooking competition. Four officers, eighteen
NCOs and regular troops were sent to Germany for
training. Planning for leave was begun, because many
soldiers had not seen their families all year.

At the end of November, the temperature fell below
–10°C during the night. On 16 November, it fell to –16°C
in the evening. We saw the first cases of frostbite, and
the doctors, assisted by Russian women, taught the men
how to treat them: delicate massage, applications of
talcum, warming the affected limb. By mid-December,
the daytime temperature had fallen to below –20°C. The
soldiers still had not received any winter clothing and
equipment.

Georg's battalion had been promised 400 pairs of skis,
which finally arrived in the middle of the winter. But
the men still had only their thin uniform jackets. In

December the whole of the 6th Division received just a few dozen pairs of fur-lined boots and overcoats. The doctors advised the men to wear all their available underclothes. This was not sufficient. The smallest gaps in the clothing were stuffed with newspaper, packaging materials and rags. Newspaper in one's pants, newspaper around one's legs and around one's thorax. Since they were receiving nothing in the way of official supplies, Georg decided to do something. He sent our friend Karl von Wendt to Westphalia, accompanied by a small team of men and trucks, with the goal of bringing back furs and warm garments.

So there was the battalion in the snow, like a marmot ready to hibernate, thinking more about holing up in a comfortable bivouac than about exposing itself to the cold, and more about celebrating Christmas than about fighting. However, December marked the beginning of the Russian counter-offensive to relieve Moscow. This strategic manoeuvre, which coincided with the entry of the United States into the conflict, clearly represented a change in the course of the war. It signalled the end of the German advance into Russian territory, even if, we thought, it was not yet decisive for the outcome of the conflict. The war would be long, German troops would turn out to be dangerously exposed and their defence system fragile, particularly under inhuman meteorological conditions.

In mid December, the situation no longer allowed the Sixth Army to maintain its bridgehead at Kalinin. The Soviet divisions, perfectly equipped, crossed the frozen Volga without difficulty and some units were able to make impressive inroads, penetrating far beyond the front lines. Several German divisions were in real danger of being surrounded and destroyed. A Siberian cold had set in: the temperature fell to -30° and -40°C. The wind blew in gusts that almost toppled the men. And when the skies cleared and a pale sun made the white desert shine with a crystal brilliance, the beauty of the countryside did not make us forget the cold, which became even more lacerating.

On 15 December, the battalion commanded by Franz-Josef von Kageneck had held, virtually alone, the road to Kalinin against forces ten times larger, and thus allowed almost a whole army to escape being surrounded. In the early morning of 16 December, Georg's reconnaissance battalion, which was under the command of the Sixth Army, was ordered to begin withdrawing to the right bank of the Volga. More unfavourable conditions could not be imagined. The storm was howling. The snow was already impressively deep when the men got up, and terrible, biting wind was raising great spumes of white powder. Drifts blocked the roads. The heavy squadron was struggling: the bad weather was trebling fuel consumption. In the early afternoon, headquarters was informed that the motorized vehicles could not continue further than 25 kilometres without additional fuel. Once again, horses constituted the only reliable motive force in a winter context. The superior officers were on the brink of despair, but young officers like Georg and Kageneck yielded less to sombre reflections. It was a matter of survival. Galvanized by the danger, they often took the initiative.

On 18 December, Georg and his men were supposed to secure a 7.5 square kilometre zone to enable the infantry to make a relatively orderly retreat from the area between the Tma and the Volga, which they had conquered at the end of October. The enemy pressure was strong, but thanks to their mobility they were able to deceive the enemy and confuse their scouts. The men had to deal not only with heavy fire but also with the cold. The gusts of wind, which were asphyxiating, burned the lungs. The cold was not only bitter, it was deadly: it could kill a man in a few minutes. If it didn't kill the man whole, it killed his limbs – hands, arms, legs – and the most prominent parts of the face – the ears and the nose. The conditions under which the retreat took place did not allow the burial of the dead. It was impossible to dig graves; instead the dead were buried under huge piles of snow. On 24 December, the temperature fell to -46°C.

That day, Siberian troops staged a mass attack on the battalion's cyclist squadron. After fighting and heavy losses among enemy forces that were still poorly equipped, it was possible to stabilize the situation. We had suffered a serious reverse. One thing reassured us: the enemy was losing on average ten to twenty times more men than we were, but we were now certain that their numbers were immense – that was their main potential. Beyond that one certainty, how many questions there were! How could the Russian generals let their men be mown down in large numbers by machine-gun fire? Why didn't they see that their counter-offensive, although it had resulted in clear successes, made no sense? In our opinion, it was a pyrrhic victory.

When Christmas came, the 6th Infantry was licking its wounds and counting its losses, which had been considerable over the past fortnight. In theory, Georg's reconnaissance battalion consisted of more than a thousand men. On 27 December, it was no more than a shadow of its former self. Georg sent his superiors a report explaining that his combat potential had been reduced by 90 per cent since June. The cavalry squadron now had only one officer, thirty-two men and four light machine guns. The heavy squadron had only twenty-nine soldiers under the command of a single officer. Finally, the lieutenant who commanded the cyclist squadron had hardly twenty-two fighters. It is true that several dozen men were on leave or in training, but since June, the dead and wounded had not been replaced. The battalion as a whole now counted only half as many troops as the *squadron* that Georg had commanded up until the spring of 1941 ... And the forces still available were exhausted, because the Soviets were attacking all the time, by day and by night.

On 29 December, the enemy launched a new offensive between the Volga and the Tma. The front line was no longer tenable, and our troops had to retreat and take up positions more to the south-west, not far from Rzhev. That city, located where the Volga begins a vast, meandering curve to the north, was an industrial centre of about 50,000 inhabitants, and especially a major railway junction. It could not be left in Russian hands. The 110th, the 126th, and the 6th Infantry Divisions gathered in this sector, where our defence was organized around what was soon to be called the Koenigsberg position.

On 1 January, Georg went to meet the 3rd Battalion of the 18th Infantry Regiment, which formed the rear guard of the retreating 6th Division. Its commandant, Kageneck, had died three days earlier. Georg found exhausted men, officers on the verge of a nervous breakdown after countless nights without sleep and weeks without rest. While the soldiers, who were not very close to the defensive line, continued their march, Georg took the officers to his command post to tell them briefly how the Koenigsberg position was organized. 'It is not an ideal front line, but it respects the tactical imperatives and has certain potentialities,' he said. 'Now, that's not all. Sit down for a moment. I've got a quart of nice hot bouillon for you,' he continued with his usual liveliness, even though the Russians were only a few kilometres away. One officer got up to serve. 'No,' Georg said, shaking his head in protest, 'I'll serve today.' That was the way my brother was, mixing rigour, lucidity and good-heartedness.

The front was being stabilized. Rzhev was finally lost in March 1943, after very fierce fighting. But until the beginning of March 1942, the Russian harassments were incessant, and their attacks came almost daily – dreadful butcheries, the unfurling of waves of men drunk on vodka and the cold, cut down by machine-gun fire, but each time reducing our troops' resistance a little. In February, a Russian cavalry division, with the help of partisans, managed to penetrate our rear and created a pocket of territory along the railway from Vyasma to

Moscow that was completely outside our control.

The situation in my sector was no better. But the story of my adventures at the turn of the year 1941–2 is briefer than that of the episodes Georg was involved in during those bloody weeks, because a wound I had received during the first hours of combat, which nearly cost me my life, sent me away from the front. Since the beginning of December, fighting had raged around Moscow, and the 86th Division had been violently torn out of its torpor. On 10 December, it was decided to retake a town called Ignatovo, which the Russians had seized. An artillery regiment had left a valuable part of its equipment there. The temperature was now 42 below zero. The cyclist squadron commanded by Lieutenant von Blomberg was to attack from the south, supported by three heavy machine guns, an anti-tank gun and a light cavalry mortar.[7] At the head of my cavalry squadron, I was assigned to lead the attack from the north. We first had to go around the village on the west and through the forest. The snow was so deep that it blocked the anti-aircraft machine gun and the cavalry artillery. Only our heavy machine gun made it to the site.

A merciless battle began that was to last several hours. The Russians resisted stubbornly. Despite the cover provided by artillery camouflaged in a nearby forest – and which unfortunately once landed a shell among our troops – we were not able to reach the houses on the village outskirts. We had to fight for a house, a fence, a vegetable garden. The enemy firepower dramatically increased and was concentrated on the north sector. This shift in the Soviet defence seemed to me inexplicable, although it was tragically simple: the German head adjutant, who was supervising the telephone connection and at the same time commanding the artillery battery, had not received the message ordering the division to retreat. The Russians, finding the pressure on their south and west flanks relieved by the departure of the cyclists, had shifted all their efforts to the cavalry squadron, which, kneeling or crawling in the snow as the light faded, persisted in a vain attempt to move forward. It was at that point that a searing pain flattened me. I had been hit in the abdomen. I did not have much time to think about my fate or even to suffer, because I lost consciousness. When I came to, I managed to stay on the battlefield for a while. The situation was becoming increasingly desperate. Grenades were exploding in the icy snow drifts, throwing up little columns of snow and powder along with bits of wood and glass. The wounded men's cries of pain, mixed with the crackling of machine-gun fire, shattered the late afternoon, and, as if through the fog of a slow nightmare, the sound managed to reach my consciousness, despite the blood I had lost, and despite the sensation of both immense weakness and a certain lightness that comes with being seriously wounded. Snow began to fall, heavy, thick and abundant, but it did not mute the din of the fighting. Soon the light machine guns began to jam. Only the horses were still going about their task, heroic, impassive, moving out damaged equipment and wounded men.

The squadron had already lost thirty-five men. I was wounded again, this time in the left shoulder. I nonetheless had the strength to give the order to retreat at nightfall. The few dozen men who were still on their feet, helped by the inexhaustible horses, hurriedly loaded up the equipment, the wounded and the frozen bodies of the dead and set out to look for the battalion, whose location they no longer knew. It seems that they walked for hours in the fresh snow, carrying me on a stretcher. The scouts were in the lead, and were sinking thigh-deep in the snow. The men were stumbling with fatigue but got up again when they came in contact with the wet snow or were scratched by the ice.

I owed my survival solely to the attention my men gave me, and to the devotion of one adjutant in particular. During the night, we ran into the battalion's doctor, who gave me first aid and dressed my wounds. 'Lieutenant,' he said, 'to have any chance of surviving, you must not eat anything for the next several days. Absolutely nothing!' He gave me a whole carton of cigarettes to ward off hunger, and loaded me on a sleigh driven by a Russian prisoner. This man, who had been captured a month earlier, was one of those Russians who viscerally rejected communism and hoped that a German victory would mean a return to the old order. For ten days he drove me over the icy plain. He was a teacher and spoke a little German, but my physical condition prevented me from conversing much with him.

At the Sysschevka railway station I was loaded – and that is the right word – into a freight train, along with forty-two other seriously wounded men. The train remained for three whole days at the station in Orel, without any care or any food being given to the wounded. The moans ceased, one by one. Half the wounded died of the cold. Aerial attacks on the station killed a number of men. However, I escaped with a piece of shrapnel in my right knee the first night, and another in my left tibia the following night. The few survivors were taken on to Smolensk. There we were transferred, in another freight train, to Germany. I had eaten practically nothing since 10 December. The train's engineer occasionally gave me a little something to drink. That was how I spent my Christmas 1941 ... Finally, after eighteen days' travel, I was taken off the train in Silesia and moved, half-dead, to the hospital in Breslau. I had survived about three weeks of transportation and privations – a miracle. Once I had recovered, I drew from all this very pessimistic conclusions regarding the ability of the military command to conduct the war.

For his part, Georg had not been seriously wounded. He was exhausted, but his morale was intact. He had, I think, lost none of his bravery, his energy, or his presence. He had never considered the situation hopeless, despite the cold, despite the adversary's firepower. With the same gaiety, he continued to give his entourage that impression of invulnerability that made him seem almost a mythical hero. Georg was perfectly well aware of the danger. But he was motivated by a sense of duty that obliged him to show, with respect to his men, a tranquil optimism. The Russian offensive had lost some of its vigour, and Georg was prepared to fight for every inch of the terrain.

But something inexplicable happened. On 10 January 1942, he received, by way of the division, the news that he had been transferred to the Führer's reserve, effective immediately. He was to return to Germany without delay. Georg had not requested this assignment. He was furious to be separated from his men, who owed him everything, but to whom he was linked by a set of obligations and loyalties that were as strong as those between a father and his children. Georg tried not to show his bitterness; on 12 January, he named his successor and left for Potsdam-Krampnitz, where he was to teach military tactics to elite troops. It is true that from an operational point of view, the cavalry had become less useful. The defensive positions the German army had taken up around Rzhev could be held by the infantry.

At the end of January, Georg and five of his comrades were decorated by the Führer in person. He was the fifty-third soldier in the Wehrmacht to receive the Knight's Cross with oak leaves. At that time he had only scorn for Hitler – not yet hatred. A photo shows the furious way my brother looked at the Führer. Hitler asked him if he had a special favour to ask. Far from thinking of himself, Georg took advantage of the opportunity: 'I have heard that my brother Philipp has been seriously wounded. I don't know where he is. Could inquiries be made at the various hospitals?'

The message was immediately sent out in all directions. When the hospital in Breslau realized that I was the wounded man being sought, the doctor came to ask me – as in a fairy tale – if I wished for anything. I was by then capable of understanding the situation, and seizing my chance, I asked to be transferred to Bonn. The Führer's desires were orders, and my wish immediately granted. So I was taken home in a luxurious railway car, surrounded by the almost maternal care of two nurses reserved for me. I spent several months in the hospital. When I got out, in spring 1942, I was still convalescent.

A few months later, in July 1942, after the training session was over, Georg was sent to Romania as part of the German military mission. He was supposed to help toughen up the Romanians, whom the Wehrmacht was then using as auxiliaries on the Russian front.

THE CONSPIRACY BEGINS
(1941–1942)

Entering a resistance movement is the result of a personal development. This process was already difficult in the territories occupied by Germany. It was all the more difficult, I think, among Germans. I had not become an officer in order to shoot the head of state like a dog. Desiring the end of the regime and the death of its leader was, in the eyes of our compatriots, not only a state offence, but also a stab in the back of the people as a whole, which was united in fighting a merciless war. The decision to join the resistance could only result from a long process, which was certainly made easier by the events, scenes, and situations I had observed or experienced. Without generalizing from my own case, there were few examples in Germany, at least among military men, of a spontaneous and impulsive commitment to the struggle against the regime. In my case, it was a combination of different experiences that led to the decision to rebel, to the point that this idea, which was at first difficult to accept, by 1942 seemed obvious and even obligatory. I was also lucky enough to meet people who were farther along in their development, and who embodied my commitment. The education Georg and I had received was certainly not alien to the evolution of our views, which advanced in tandem even though we had been separated in 1941–2 and our communications on this subject were, necessarily, fleeting.

What was our state of mind before we became aware of the need to act? Here is an example taken from June 1941, in the middle of the offensive. My unit was stationed somewhere on the right bank of the Dnieper. Late one evening, I began talking with an artillery lieutenant who was passing through and to whom I had offered my hospitality. It was one of those long conversations, frequent among officers, that take place over a last cup of coffee or a glass of liqueur, and in which one speaks about one's feelings, one's hopes and also one's fears. Our conversation turned to the Nazis, and more precisely to Hitler. Feeling that we were in agreement on the subject, and emboldened by some feeling of mutual trust, by fatigue, and perhaps by a little alcohol, we began to criticize the Führer. We talked about this and that, while the fire burned down. The embers were glowing, and it grew colder. One of us yawned, thus putting an end to the discussion as spontaneously as we had begun it.

We wished each other good night and went back to our tents. I suddenly broke out in a cold sweat. Who was this fellow with whom I had spoken a bit too frankly? I didn't know him; he belonged to another division, and an artillery division to boot. How could I be sure of his discretion? On the contrary, he had given me every reason to think that he liked to talk. How could I assure myself of his loyalty? Impossible. The army, like all of German society after eight years of dictatorship, was full of informers, swarms of zealous agents loyal to the system. This fellow with a friendly face could very easily betray the feelings of confidence he inspired. Thinking, expressing doubts, mocking the Führer, questioning the meaning of this ideological war was already a crime. My doubt became anguish, and fear yielded to panic. I didn't sleep a wink all night. The following day, I did not attempt to see this dangerous fellow again.

However, I ran across him a few months later. In the meantime I had learned that he was Achim Oster, the son of Hans Oster, the number two man in the German counter-espionage service (Abwehr), and the keystone of the resistance movements.[8]

'If you only knew how scared I was!' I told him when we had recognized each other.

'And what about me? I didn't sleep all night!'

We laughed a great deal about it, showing how much officers were tempted to express their bitterness in private, despite the danger of doing so, even outside the Nazi apparatus.

At the same time, Georg found himself, according to his comrades, in a similar state of mind. By the end of August 1941, the effects of the disastrous hygienic conditions that had been endured for ten weeks were beginning to make themselves felt among his troops. Exhausted by too little sleep, confronted by extreme weather conditions, harassed by marches and battles, attacked by lice and mosquitoes, prevented from doing laundry regularly, dozens of men in the 6th Reconnaissance Battalion were beginning to show the symptoms of dysentery. Despite the strict instructions given by the doctors – drink boiled water and nothing else – the men's bodies, of which too much had been demanded, became vulnerable. Repeated vaccinations carried out in early August against all sorts of epidemics were not sufficient. The weather, which had been so good in early July, had deteriorated. The coolness and humidity at the end of the summer led to cramps and rheumatism among even the toughest of the men. These joint pains, which were soon accompanied by gastric problems and weight loss, were the early signs of dreadful diarrhoeas. In short, on 26 August, in Georg's cavalry squadron alone, thirty-two men had already fallen sick and were incapable of fighting. Dr Haape, the doctor for the neighbouring 18th Infantry Regiment, tried to treat every new case. Georg was ill, even though he refused to be put on the sick list. However, he consented to have himself treated for a week by Dr Haape, to take laxatives, and even – the greatest shame – to stay in bed for days with a hot-water bottle on his stomach. To thank the doctor, who was indefatigably performing his duties, Georg, who had recovered after eight days under his care, invited him to dinner along with Franz-Joseph Kageneck. They began to talk about this and that. The conversation then turned to more serious subjects. Georg felt at ease talking with Haape, whose humanity appeared on his round and jovial face, and with Kageneck, who was a military man par excellence, a Catholic – he came from a family in Baden that included Metternich's mother – and irreproachably upright. Soon, Georg gave free rein to his anger against Hitler:

'That obtuse parvenu! He's a cheap café politician

pretending to be a genius!' he suddenly exploded. 'Why didn't he stay in the background and let the generals think for him?'

'Because he is inspired,' Kageneck said slowly.

'Do you know what inspiration is?' Haape asked. 'It's an intestinal wind that rises by mistake to the head and lodges there – and that's Immanuel Kant's definition, not mine!'

'We can't go on much longer considering him and his illuminations to be just a joke,' Georg grumbled, without even smiling at the doctor's quip.

The criticism Georg formulated was in fact already quite common among military officers. But Georg went much further. Lowering his voice and leaning over the table, he added (Haape tells us):

'The Nazis are destroying the heart of the true Germany! When the war is over, it will be people like us who will have to act!'

'But whom will you have to help you?' Kageneck asked doubtfully.

'Most of the generals! From all these discussions something will eventually materialize – particularly if we have to suffer defeats.'

'Generals don't make an army,' Kageneck interrupted. 'You know as well as I do that most of the young officers coming in are confirmed Nazis.'

'And what about the troops?' Haape added. 'Most of them are happy just to have a place to lay their heads and sleep, and their rations three times a day! They won't do anything. They don't care whether they are fighting for the true Germany or Hitler's Germany . . .'

Georg was not one of those who acknowledge their doubts, who resolutely question themselves, who sound out their fellows, who probe the depths of their thoughts and ask others to confirm them ... When he expressed himself, he had already made up his mind. His friends had pointed out the practical difficulties involved in what he proposed to do. Their objections gave him food for thought, particularly regarding the generals' involvement. But he was already fully committed to his enterprise, even if its exact outlines were not yet clearly determined.

Fifteen months later, Tresckow enlisted Georg among the opponents and conspirators of the Army Group Centre. In the meantime, his opinion of Hitler had become more radical, to the point that in his view it was not possible to wait until the end of the war to eliminate him.

I cannot reconstitute the reasoning that led him to this conclusion, the totality of the feelings, analyses, images and impressions that moved him to take this decisive step. But it is clear that Georg's assignments, starting in early 1942, left him time to observe and meditate. Chance – some would say Providence – had provided him with this strange interlude, this inexplicable parenthesis in a life that up to then had always tended toward action. Established 70 kilometres north of Bucharest, he was the only German among a population that was almost entirely Romanian. In his letters to a woman friend of ours, he described his occupations: 'My activity here is not very exciting. I work at the officer training school, where I serve as a supervisor and offer advice regarding the best training methods. The Romanians are extremely sensitive, and one must therefore always be very careful. In other respects, they are very hospitable, and we get along very well. I am trying to train a young dog who is excessively fearful – one of my bitch's puppies. Not ideal for here, because for big game one obviously needs a somewhat more aggressive dog.'[9] Later he added, 'I've quite a lot of time for reflection and writing.'[10] Georg was in regular contact with the front – by mail, first of all, since the postal service was still working well – because people were in the habit of writing to each other often, not only within the family, but also among fellow officers. We also communicated by telephone. I could in fact be reached quite easily, given my service to Marshal Kluge. And I communicated to Georg all the information in my possession that proceeded from the various divisions. This news, put into perspective during his long periods of leisure, increased his scepticism.

In my own journey the inevitable and the predestined probably played a role. In retrospect, my involvement may seem to have been governed by a logical sequence, but I have to admit that it depended to a great extent on fortuitous circumstances. If I hadn't been wounded in December 1941, if I hadn't been assigned to Kluge's staff, if I hadn't met Tresckow, that exceptional figure, and especially if I hadn't acquired the habit of confiding some of my thoughts to him, I would never have emerged from my reserve. I would have remained captive to private scruples and irresoluble internal conflicts. To begin this intellectual and moral development was to embark upon a pilgrimage whose goal was uncertain. It was already to commit treason. To be sure, Hitler had failed many a time to keep his word, and he had sacrificed tens of thousands of lives to his diabolical whims. Nonetheless, for a military man, for whom the first requirement was obedience, starting down this road was certainly not easy.

During this period I was very busy, certainly, but I also had time to discuss things with other officers, to meditate on the course of events and the regime's goals. That is how a kind of maturation took place in me before more decisive experiences thrust me into active military resistance. Among soldiers, there was much discussion of the sermons that Mgr von Galen, the bishop of Münster, had given against euthanasia almost a year earlier, in the summer of 1941, and whose vehemence had led the government, contrary to all expectations, to put an end to the T4 programme – a programme for the eradication of the handicapped. These sermons had resonated with soldiers, who are always likely, after a wound or an amputation, to be grouped together with those allegedly useless people. I had not read the sermons, but I had heard many people talk about them, and I had listened all the more attentively because Mgr von Galen, without being a close relative – we were distant cousins – was a compatriot. The bishop was highly regarded among officers who had any sense of morality and his influence on resistance in the military can be seen in a brief exchange I had with Colonel Hans Oster of the intelligence services toward the end of 1942. Knowing my connection to the Rhineland and Westphalia, and although he was himself a Lutheran, he asked me about the prelate:

'Are you a relative of Mgr von Galen?'

'No, not really . . .'

'Too bad. He's a man of courage and conviction. And what resolution in his sermons! There should be a handful of such people in all our churches, and at least two handfuls in the Wehrmacht! If there were, Germany would look quite different!'

In this context, certain incidents led me to enter the conspiracy. In retrospect, compared with the horror of the war and the magnitude of the Nazis' crimes, these incidents seem minor. Another person might have reacted coolly to these experiences, and not been affected by them. But for me, they served as a catalyst. It is time to write about them.

AN ENCOUNTER WITH THE DEMON
(JUNE 1942)

By early May 1942, I had largely recovered from my wound, but I remained handicapped. Limping, unable to ride a horse, I could not resume an operational assignment. I was therefore attached to the staff of the Army Group Centre, as an aide-de-camp to Field Marshal von Kluge. My role, like that of aides-de-camp in every army in the world, oscillated between all-purpose maid and office manager: handling the marshal's schedule, accompanying him, participating in discussions, writing up reports on meetings, summarizing the dispatches and radio messages that had come in overnight so they could be read in the early morning, running errands, transmitting orders, and, in short, organizing the marshal's material life in order to facilitate his direction of operations. Kluge did not mistreat me. On the contrary, he was concerned to make full use of my abilities. The marshal, who was overloaded if anyone ever was, often asked me to write the orders for the following day – a function that obviously belonged to the operations officer, that is, Tresckow. The next day, the marshal compared Tresckow's orders with mine, and to train me he pointed out my errors and their possible consequences ... In the afternoon, when nothing special was planned, we took tea together. In the evening, I accompanied him on his walks. I had, in a way, become the confidant of this old military man, who was a very interesting person.

I was lodged in the same group of huts as Kluge, along with the chief of staff, Wöhler, and the service personnel (the orderly, the cook, and the driver), while the rest of the staff lived in a barracks about 300 metres away. We went on duty at 6 a.m. At that hour, we received the 'night bulletin' from the staff's operations office. I was supposed to present it to the marshal at exactly seven o'clock. During the first weeks, I found this exercise very difficult. On his 1/300,000 map, Kluge had marked only the front, with a thick, dark line. He had not indicated the limits of the respective sectors held by the divisions. At that time the Army Group Centre included ninety divisions, and I was supposed to indicate, using a long wand, exactly where the night's battles – thrusts, captures, attacks – took place, and continue my analysis down to the level of the regiment and the village. Fortunately, I had good eyes. After this presentation came breakfast, which the marshal and I always ate separately, whereas we shared the other meals with the marshal's staff. In the course of the morning, General Wöhler, the head of staff, Tresckow, the operations officer (Ia), the intelligence officer (Ic), and other department heads on the staff came in to report. That was the schedule on sedentary days. However, weather permitting, we took the plane several times a week to inspect the terrain. Then it was the local staff's turn to make their reports. Kluge took advantage of this opportunity to visit frontline units that were directly exposed to the enemy.

The first incident occurred a few days after my arrival at the marshal's headquarters, probably in June 1942, though I am unable to determine the exact date. Until I was wounded, I had always been in advanced positions, assigned to operational duties. I had not had an opportunity to observe what was happening in the areas of the East that were not under military command, and where the general commissioner, the SS, and the Sicherheits-Dienst (SD) exercised a limitless authority. The military had in fact authority over the front – hundreds of kilometres long – and a zone 200 to 300 kilometres wide constituting the army's rear (*rückwärtiges Heeresgebiet*). Between that zone and Germany's borders was the buffer zone under the control of the infamous Reichs-kommissariat Ost. In the territory under military command, the SS were authorized to act only in the framework of the battle against partisans. This accommodation with the Nazi universe might seem to be a criminal weakness, a cowardly pliability on the part of a hypocritical military hierarchy, which was blind and mute. But the partisans were conducting a merciless guerrilla war in the rear areas. Ambushes, attacks on food supply convoys, massacres of columns of wounded men as they were being taken to the hospital, terrorist actions in villages and farms that had supported us or simply offered us lodging, infiltration of spies along the front lines, sometimes even within the families where the Wehrmacht's soldiers were billeted: all that not only threatened to disrupt the front, but especially to lead to a breakdown of the army's supply system, which was already extremely vulnerable.

One fine day in the spring, therefore, I received one of the many dispatches I was supposed to summarize for the marshal. This one came from the SS Obergruppenführer Erich von dem Bach-Zelewski. It concerned the rear zone that was beyond military control but concerned the staff of the Army Group of the Centre because it provided information on the actions the partisans had carried out against roads, viaducts and bridges that had an obvious strategic importance. The message ended with a fifth point, under what seemed to me an enigmatic and vaguely troubling entry: 'Special treatment for five Gypsies.' I couldn't grasp the relation between this point and the other rubrics in the message. A few hours later, I submitted my report to the marshal. I came to the fifth point.

'Marshal, I cannot explain the meaning of this expression to you.'

The marshal replied: 'Frankly, I don't know what to tell you. We have to clarify this matter. The simplest way will be to ask Bach-Zelewski for further details. I happen to have a meeting with him in a few days.'

Erich von dem Bach-Zelewski was not a harmless person. People trembled at the mere mention of his name. He was in his forties, a massive, rather ordinary-looking man. He was very experienced in military affairs and no one could accuse him of incompetence in that domain. But his service record did not inspire respect. Having entered the army when he was very young, during the last years of the Great War, in 1918–19 he had allowed himself to be drawn into the activities of the *Freikorps*. There he had lost his values and even the slightest sense of humanity.[11] Since June 1941 he had been high commandant of the SS and the police (Höherer SS- und Polizeiführer) in the central Russia sector. He reigned like a satrap over a sinister empire that included Minsk and Mogilev. Ruthless, coldly calculating, he was truly a creature of the Devil.[12]

Among the officers, Bach-Zelewski had a scandalous reputation as an unscrupulous careerist who was full of bitterness against the military men who had expelled him from the army fifteen years earlier. In spring 1942, news of the atrocities committed by his henchmen had not yet spread beyond the limited group of eye-witnesses. Moreover, in the sulphurous rumours that swirled about him, it was hard to distinguish fiction from reality. But he had been assigned to carry on the battle against the partisans that the regular army, which was busy holding the front, could not handle. Erich von dem Bach-Zelewski was an unavoidable partner.

I was present at the discussion between Bach-Zelewski and Kluge. They talked first about the guerrillas, how to limit their range, how to eliminate them from the countryside, and especially how to secure the vital connections with Germany. A discreet reminder on my part, once the technical presentation was complete, caused Kluge rather abruptly to ask the SS officer: 'Oh, by the way, I nearly forgot: what do you mean in your report by "special treatment?" You apparently gave "special treatment" to five Gypsies.'

'Those? We shot them!'

'What do you mean, shot them! After a trial before a military tribunal?'

'No, of course not! All the Jews and Gypsies we pick up are liquidated, shot!'

The marshal and I were both taken aback. I felt the kind of internal dislocation and annihilation that leads to panic fear. Obviously, we sensed that something was wrong. Kluge could not have been unaware that crimes, major crimes, had been committed. We still attributed them to the uncontrolled excesses of the SS. But here was Bach-Zelewski stating a doctrine of extermination as though it were perfectly natural. What we had thought were terrible blunders were in reality part of a coherent, premeditated plan. The shooting of Jews and Gypsies turned out to be a commonly shared war goal. According to the SS, the instructions were clear and came from the highest level of the government. The marshal got a grip on himself and controlled the trembling of his voice: 'But why did you shoot them? You're only creating new partisans by killing them like that. It's incredible! Are you really executing them outside the military code of procedure, without trial?'

The atmosphere became more heated. The old marshal, even though he was used to dealing with Nazi high officials, was on the verge of exploding. The placid coolness of our interlocutor, his quiet hatred, and simply his way of expressing his murderous obsession so calmly may have enraged the marshal even more than the fate of the five unfortunate Gypsies. Overwhelmed by anger, and no doubt emboldened by my presence, he protested in the name of the Geneva conventions, the laws of war, and even the interest of the German armies. Bach-Zelewski grew angry as well. Pale, his eyes piercing behind his round tortoise-shell spectacles, his expression, which a moment before had been unctuous, hardened. After a few minutes he put an end to the dispute with these dreadful words: 'Jews and Gypsies are among the Reich's enemies. We have to liquidate them.' And he added, his myopic eyes fixed on Kluge, without any regard for his rank or function: 'Yes, all the enemies of the Reich, our mission is to liquidate them!'

The threat was thinly veiled. The SS officer turned on his heel and left.

Kluge was not a man to temporize. He immediately called General Halder of the Army General Staff. Leaving aside pointless humanitarian or legal arguments, Kluge tried to prove the inanity of this enterprise, which stiffened resistance instead of breaking it. The only positive result of his energetic complaints was that we no longer heard about Bach-Zelewski. Perhaps he simply stopped reporting his barbaric acts.[13]

This incident changed my view of the war. I was disgusted and afraid. I had already had occasion to wonder about the meaning of this conflict, its strategic pertinence, and the Führer's tactics. Through friends in my division's reserve battalion who had been sent to Stargard[14] shortly after the invasion of Poland, I had heard rumours about the crimes committed by the SS in the areas conquered. We were surprised not so much by these rumours – there were so many young men with morals in the SS units – as by the perpetrators' complete immunity, telling ourselves that this could not go on for long. In any case, we considered these atrocities, which were probable but never proven, to be isolated events.

Henceforth, I had the proof of the abomination before my eyes. It was no longer a matter of isolated acts committed by aberrant individuals. It was a rigorous plan that had been sanctioned by the highest authorities. We had to face the facts: the state, as a whole, was riddled with vice and crime. And the army, by remaining silent, was making itself the system's accomplice. This situation now seems to us blindingly clear. It was not so clear for contemporaries, who were convinced that Germany was a model of civilization, and that it could not be subjected to either a dictatorship or a murderous totalitarianism.

For several weeks, I remained in a state of deep perplexity. I reported the incident to Tresckow, in whom I liked to confide. But then what should be done? Speak out? To whom? To say what? To denounce the perpetrators? To whom? And according to what criteria? The scales of value had been corrupted: the altercation with Bach-Zelewski had shown clearly enough how the fruit had already been eaten away from the inside.

From then on, I paid more attention to conversations among officers and to allusions I could now decode, and I noticed that people within the staff knew about the execution of the Jews. It was mentioned covertly, with repugnance, and the blame was put on foreign recruits in the SS. One fact in particular was evident, since members of the staff of the Army Group Centre had witnessed it directly. In October 1941, in Borissov, Latvian SS-men had executed thousands of Jews and thrown them into a giant ditch. By chance, two superior officers, Carl-Hans von Hardenberg and Heinrich von Lehndorff, had seen the massacre. Because of bad weather, the plane carrying them was flying at low altitude and the two men had seen every detail of this nightmare. Hardenberg, who was then the private aide-de-camp to Marshal Fedor von Bock, the commander-in-chief of the Army Group Centre, had appealed to his superior. The local military commandant was immediately summoned. How could he have allowed such crimes to be committed on the territory for which he was responsible? He would have to answer for this massacre of the innocents. The commandant, confronted with his own cowardice and racked with remorse, committed suicide. This affair caused two of the principal officers of the staff, Tresckow and Gersdorff, to join the resistance to Hitler. In the spring of 1942, I was still unaware of this radicalization among my great friends, their state of mind, and the double game they were playing.

I soon had another example of the lethal effect of the prejudices held by the masters of Germany with regard to allegedly inferior races. Tresckow had convinced Kluge to send to the Führer a small delegation of Ukrainians who had gone over to the Germans and wanted to set up a buffer state with its own army. Hitler refused to receive them and had the unfortunate delegates immediately shot.

An Incident at the Führer's Headquarters
(July 1942)

The second incident took place in the Führer's head-quarters in Vinnytsia,[15] in Ukraine. For very important matters, the marshal called upon the commander-in-chief. In early summer 1942 the critical situation in the Rzhev Gap justified a request for an audience. Since 1 August, Rzhev had been under attack by several hundred thousand men. The preceding July, the German army had purged the south-west sector of this region of the last Russian elements that had been infiltrated there. The feeling of security did not last. The Soviets, now helped by the Americans, were using unprecedented firepower. The Ninth Army under General Model was now in serious danger of being surrounded – a real mousetrap. Within the structure of Army Group Centre, the Ninth occupied an important place. Kluge, fearing that it would be completely destroyed, urged that certain positions considered non-strategic be abandoned, that the front line be shortened to make it more defensible, and especially that the troops that had been fighting non-stop since June 1941 be relieved, in order to give them a little rest in the rear area and allow them to rebuild their strength. The conversation had been care-fully prepared, with a series of arguments, information sheets for the presentation, and so on. I was all the more involved in the question because I had several friends and cherished cousins in that sector. It was a matter of life and death for my old comrades in the 86th Division, and also for my brother Georg's comrades in the famous 6th Reconnaissance Battalion, which was caught in the same net. Early on the morning of 9 August we flew to Vinnytsia.

For the first time, I was not allowed to take part in the discussion. At lunch, I was separated from Kluge. While he sat at the Führer's table, I was placed at Martin Bormann's. Bormann was the head of the party and the Führer's partner in crime. Brutal, careless, violent, he was a man who immediately inspired fear: that was my first impression. At the table were seated representatives of all the ministries. Although I was surrounded by men in various uniforms, I was one of the genuine military men present. These gaudy outfits and tinny decorations seemed to me worthy of a decadent royal court. What I heard of the conversations was so dreadfully banal that I remember it perfectly.

Soon after the meal began, the representative of the Foreign Ministry, who wore an elaborate dress uniform, asked Bormann what should be done in the following case: Archduke Joseph, an Austrian marshal, was about to celebrate his seventieth birthday. Should a con-gratulatory telegram be sent to him? The diplomat pointed out that the marshal had nonetheless married a Wittelsbach, that is, a Bavarian Catholic (he seemed not to realize that the Habsburgs themselves were Catholic).

Bormann peremptorily issued his verdict: 'Catholic? Then he won't get his telegram!'

The representative of the Ministry of Agriculture asked Bormann what would happen to the former kolkhozes that specialized in growing koksagys, a local variety of dandelion whose roots could theoretically produce a rubber substitute. Scientific studies would have to be done to confirm the value of growing it. Half-seriously, Bormann immediately passed the buck, saying only: 'That's a matter for Reichsführer Himmler!'

At dessert, some of these gentlemen complained that fresh strawberries were already unavailable in the Führer's headquarters, so that they had had to resort to cherries – which were unpleasant because they had pits. Finally, a few of them who'd drunk a little too much asked in loud voices who wanted to go that evening to provide gallant company for the girls in the Kraft durch Freude group that was visiting Vinnytsia.

That was too much for me. The gravity of the fate of the Ninth Army was confronted with moral and intellectual poverty and a disconcerting futility. Without a word, boiling with rage, I left the table and went out to smoke a cigarette to calm down. A few moments later, an aide-de-camp stuck his head out to tell me that 'Reichsleiter Bormann is asking for you'.

Coffee and liqueurs were being served. Bormann asked me to explain what I had done. I told him how I felt: 'As a lieutenant and aide-de-camp to Marshal von Kluge, I had imagined the Führer's headquarters differently. I accompanied the marshal to discuss the tragic fate of the Ninth Army, which is surrounded at Rzhev, and here people are talking about strawberries!' My frankness, though clothed in politeness, did not please Bormann. Without answering, he turned around and called hoarsely to an SS-man: 'Take this guy away.' I was locked up nearby in a small room, almost a cell. I thought of the episode in the garage in Bonn, ten years earlier. What was going to happen now? I lit another cigarette.

Having finished his lunch, Kluge was already preparing to leave, in a state of irritation not unlike my own. He came out of the mess hall and looked around for me. I heard him calling me. The guard posted outside the room finally whispered something to the marshal, thereby betraying his boss. Pushing the SS-man aside, Kluge tore open the door: 'What are you doing there?' I stammered a few words. The marshal interrupted me. 'You'll tell me all about it in the plane. Come on, out of there, we're leaving!' We quickly got into the car, which took us to the aerodrome. During the flight, I told him about my marvellous half-day. Kluge concluded: 'That's enough, that's enough. This time I was able to save you. The next time, you'll keep your mouth shut. But basically, you're absolutely right!'

A POISONED GIFT
(OCTOBER 1942)

My misadventure in Vinnytsia had proven instructive. However, I was constantly asking myself: what could I do, as a young subordinate officer, and one without operational duties? What could I do alone, without support? The answer was to come by itself two months later.

It was 29 October 1942. Hitler called the marshal, as he often did. I was at my post in the aide-de-camp's office, which was next to the marshal's. I picked up my receiver in order to listen in on the conversation. This was not an indiscretion on my part: I was supposed to listen in on telephone conversations in order to offer my impressions to the marshal and to ensure that there was no misunderstanding. This systematic monitoring shows the degree of mistrust that existed between Hitler and his generals.

As commander-in-chief, Hitler liked to give his instructions directly to the marshals. Eager for revenge, the little ex-corporal from 1918 wanted to pit his tactical genius against the excessively academic thought of the military professionals. He wanted to tear them away from what he considered to be comfortable certainties, which he regarded as mediocre and routine-bound. He despised them, but he needed their expertise and their obedience. Thus the conversations were always animated by an almost electrical tension. Kluge's operational considerations, which followed a rather classical schema, collided with the Führer's implausible strategic designs – the technician vs. the amateur, the practical man vs. the ruthless aesthete. Kluge never minced words; Hitler sometimes gave his anger free rein. I often believed that when the conversation was over Kluge would be relieved of his office. However, at the last moment, Hitler, with Machiavellian cleverness, managed to avoid a definitive rupture and reduced the tension by an adroit pirouette – a sudden change of subject, a personal compliment, and so on. The monster turned the situation around with acrobatic agility. 'Oh, by the way,' he would say for example, 'I've had your wife sent a bouquet of her favourite flowers, with my best wishes for her birthday. As for the rest, I'll call you back later.' Finishing the conversation on an almost friendly note, the dictator then made his decision in private, without consulting anyone else, because he was commander-in-chief.

This time, Hitler was calling simply to congratulate the marshal on the occasion of his birthday, which was the following day. He concluded this way: 'Marshal, I've heard that you intend to have stables built at Böhne.[16] In consideration of the many services you have rendered to the German people and to me personally, I'm giving you 250,000 marks to buy construction materials! Happy birthday and good-bye!'

'Heil, mein Führer,' the marshal replied automatically. But Hitler had already hung up. The gift was sumptuous. In a Germany that was completely focused on the war, it was extremely difficult to procure construction materials, especially since 1941 and the beginning of extensive air attacks on German cities, where daily destruction increased the need for wood, cement, and bricks.

The bell rang in my room. I went into Kluge's office. Obviously embarrassed that I had listened to this conversation, he asked:

'You heard what the Führer said at the end of his call. Just between us, what do you think about it?'

Despite my efforts to get along with my superior – I was still only twenty-five years old – I answered the sixty-year-old man somewhat coolly: 'Marshal, I admit that I don't recall that any Prussian marshal ever accepted a gift from a sovereign in the course of a campaign. After a victory, yes. But during a conflict, never. If I were you, Marshal, I would give the money to the Red Cross.'

Suddenly embarrassed by my temerity, I took my leave of the marshal, who was stunned. I was afraid that he might bring up this incident later, especially at tea-time, but he didn't. When we had finished our tea, I went, pensively, to the officer's wing of the staff headquarters. Had I exceeded the limits of an aide-de-camp's freedom? I asked to see Tresckow. I knew that I could confide in and almost confess to the staff's first officer, whose human qualities and good sense invited that sort of thing. Tresckow was a discreet man; he would not talk to others about the incident. The staff's workroom was full of people. We retired to a small room next door, where maps were kept. I told him about what had happened and asked his advice, for I had no doubt that the marshal would return to this telephone conversation when we were alone again.

The reaction of Tresckow, who was almost as upset as I was, surprised me. My astonishment grew when he asked my permission to speak with the marshal. I protested energetically. Impossible. I knew secrets that I had to protect. We got unusually testy with each other: 'Colonel,' I said, 'I'm an orderly attached to the personal service of Marshal Kluge. This is a position that requires absolute discretion. You cannot mention our conversation. I came to you as an experienced counsellor, not as my superior. Furthermore, the marshal is my only superior.'

Tresckow looked at me with a serious air. After a moment's silence, he said to me in a penetrating voice, weighing his two short sentences and speaking slowly in order to be sure he was understood: 'The marshal must not make himself dependent on the Führer. We need him in our fight against Hitler.' With these few words, Tresckow had unveiled himself. He had at the same time enlisted me in his group of conspirators. I couldn't go backwards. He left me no choice. Several times, waiting outside Kluge's office before the morning briefings, we had occasion to exchange double entendres, and he was able to test my mental dispositions. These two very simple sentences now demanded absolute confidence of me.

My heart expanded. Filled with an immense feeling of relief, I knew in whom I could confide, and with whom I could act. I was dazed, intoxicated by the confidence of this superior officer whose prudence, intelligence and shrewdness I admired. Tresckow had wrenched me out of the spiral of silence, remorse, fear and disgust. The filth and blood of the war were no longer my sole horizon. I found hope again.

The next day, Kluge received the staff to celebrate his sixtieth birthday. Assuming that word of the affair might have got out, he put it at the centre of the conversation: 'What do you think about this little "tip"?' Major-General Krebs saw no problem in accepting the gift as an equivalent of the fiefs granted under the Empire.

Tresckow warned Kluge, imploring him: 'I beg you, Marshal, don't accept a penny!'

I repeated my suggestion regarding the Red Cross. I don't know what the marshal decided in the end.

I never considered for an instant not telling Georg about all this. We were too close. But I had to hold my tongue for a long time. He was in Romania. Correspondence was subjected to aleatory censorship. The telephone worked well, but it was not secure. I had to wait until we could see each other. This opportunity came at the end of 1942.

THE TRESCKOW GROUP
(1942–1944)

Tresckow was a Prussian Protestant, an officer and the son of an officer. His vigorous soul, of spotless moral rectitude, radiated from an internal peace that put its stamp on his whole way of being. The strength of his personality, imbued with an authentic and unostentatious piety, was naturally conveyed to his entourage. Rigorous with himself, but not austere with others, Tresckow had not confined himself to a great estate or the Reichswehr's bunkers. His professional experience in banking and his residence in Latin America in the 1920s had given him an openness of mind that was rare in his milieu. He was a generous man. His presence in a group exercised a natural force of attraction, a magnetism. He never forced people to go along with him; they came spontaneously, of their own accord. He was one of those rare individuals who combine kindness, intelligence and effectiveness.

The experience of war and the nearness of death had not made him an excessively hardened man. He expressed his feelings modestly, loved nature, and was constantly admiring the work of his Creator. One day, we had gone hunting together at dawn. The first rays of sunlight were slowly dissipating the darkness, and the milky clouds were tinted a very pale pink. Nature, in the freshness of dawn, had taken on the first colours of autumn. We heard the hoarse, spell-binding belling of the stag. Then came the nuptial song of the woodcock, and his proud, grotesque strutting. I aimed my rifle. Tresckow put his hand on my shoulder, stopping me. We took the time to inhale deeply the early morning air, to contemplate nature's preparations and to listen to the strange melodies of the animal world. We started out again in pursuit of a woodcock, then stopped to silently observe multicoloured jays hopping around in the great, shady mass of the drowsy forest.

It is difficult to describe a man's faith without descending into hagiographical platitudes. Henning von Tresckow was inhabited by an ardent piety that he was not afraid to express. For Christmas 1942, the general command of the Wehrmacht had forbidden any celebration. Nazi officers had been assigned to see to it that this injunction was respected. Thus the audience was surprised when Tresckow came silently forward among his men, flanked by Schulze-Büttger and Oertzen. The operations officer read the Christmas gospel just as he would have done amidst his own family. I had informed Kluge of what Tresckow was going to do. Thus the marshal had come to the subordinate officers' mess solely to provide cover for his subordinate. It was a true Christian Christmas, to the joy of the great majority of the men.

Tresckow had a philosopher's forehead, meditative eyes and an artist's hands. This soldier loved peace, because he knew what war was. He had tasted its bitterness in 1917, when he enlisted as a cadet at the age of sixteen. In June 1918, he had gone to the front in France as a second lieutenant in the Imperial Guard's prestigious 1st Regiment of Foot. During the deadly retreat, he had contemplated the people's distress in the combat zones. After the war was over, he had to readapt to civilian life, still with the same appetite for discovery. As the operations officer on the staff of the Army Group Centre since early summer 1941, he had seen the proof of inconceivable atrocities piling up on his desk. Too much concordant evidence had transformed into an unshakeable resolution the vague project that he had envisaged as early as 1939: to kill Hitler. At first fleeting, then insistent, the idea that it was up to him to take the initiative had become a conviction. If some generals were ready to act, others, although tempted by the military adventure, were paralysed by the Prussian tradition of obedience to the monarch.

Tresckow had thus resolved to count on himself and on younger officers to decapitate the regime. Without overestimating his abilities, he knew he was capable of being both the architect and the brains of the operation, but he needed helpers. He had tried in vain to get his uncle, Marshal Fedor von Bock, the commandant of Army Group South, to join him. He had also struck higher up, in the circle of his acquaintances, beginning with Gersdorff. Since the beginning of the 1941 campaign, the two men had talked quite freely. Gersdorff was the staff's intelligence officer; in regular contact with the intelligence services in Berlin, towards which a nebulous group of opponents led by Admiral Canaris and

Colonel Oster gravitated, and he was able to complete his knowledge of the massacres, counting up the victims and transmitting these figures to Tresckow and their Berlin counterparts.

Among the subordinate officers, Fabian von Schlabrendorff was, I think, the first one approached. He was Tresckow's aide-de-camp, his cousin, and five years younger than he. A lawyer and the son of a general, he knew what law and justice are. At family reunions held before the war, he had shared with Tresckow his conviction that Germany had to be rid of tyrants. His intransigent nature, coupled with a rather contrary spirit, naturally led him into the resistance. He and Tresckow formed a complementary pair: if Tresckow was the soldier full of humanity, Schlabrendorff typified the man of law, the civilian in uniform – a uniform that was, moreover, frequently in slight disarray. A courtroom duellist with a sharp tongue, tenacious, caustic sometimes to the point of cruelty, he was not afraid to make his interlocutor blush or even to wound him. But his intellectual's spectacles and the quibbler's chatter could not hide his heart and the freedom of conscience nourished by his faith in God. The austere Schlabrendorff was to display an exemplary fidelity to all of us, even under torture.

It had been easy to approach Georg Schulze-Büttger, because his post as responsible for operations on the staff made him Tresckow's closest collaborator. Schubü – his universally adopted nickname – was an ardently religious Protestant. An indefatigable worker who was endowed with an unfailing sense of humour, he was a precious

Philipp and his brothers and sisters in front of the family home: he is the fifth from the left, in front of Georg. (Boeselager collection)

Philipp at the age of nine, with one of his father's hunting trophies, September 1926. (Boeselager collection)

RIGHT Berlin, 29 September 1938: the Paderborn 15th Cavalry Regiment parades in honour of Mussolini. Georg is leading the detachment, and Philipp is the last on the right in the first row. (Boeselager collection)

January 1942, Hitler decorates German officers at his headquarters at Rastenburg, East Prussia. From left to right: Hans Jordan, Karl Eibl, Günter Hoffmann-Schönbron, Georg Boeselager and Karl-Heinz Noak. This episode allowed Philipp to be transferred to a western German hospital after his severe wounding in December 1941. (Ullstein Bild)

LEFT Headquarters of
Army Group Centre,
summer 1942: Philipp,
seated, carries out
his functions as an
orderly; on the left,
standing, is Captain von
Bülow. (Collection
Boeselager)

Kluge's office in
Smolensk. (Collection
Boeselager)

July 1942: Kluge in the field. Philipp is on the right. (Collection Boeselager)

ABOVE The staff of Army Group Centre depart for a visit to the field (September 1942). General Wöhler is standing, Field Marshal von Kluge is sitting in the front passenger seat. Philipp is on the back seat, in the centre. (Collection Boeselager)

LEFT The officers' dining room where the plan to shoot Hitler with pistols in March 1943 was to have been carried out. (Collection Boeselager)

Operations briefing, Russia, July 1943. Georg is in the centre, Philipp on the left. (Collection Boeselager)

LEFT 2 August 1944: Georg presents his brother an Iron Cross, First Class. (Collection Boeselager)

ABOVE The two brothers with their comrades from the 3rd Cavalry Brigade. (Collection Boeselager)

With Lieutenant Schulte at Patrykozy (15km north of the Second Army headquarters at Petrikow), 1944. (Collection Boeselager)

Tresckow, Georg and Oertzen.
All three would die in the
summer of 1944. (Collection
Boeselager)

Philipp in May 1945.
(Collection Boeselager)

9 July 2004.
(Getty Images)

20 July 2004: with his wife,
Rosy, at the Ploetzensee
memorial in Berlin.
(Getty Images)

member of Tresckow's group; in fact, he had been aide-de-camp to General Beck, the former head of the Army General Staff who had resigned in 1938, and we envisaged him playing a key role if the coup d'état ever succeeded.

The group was then enlarged by successive recruitments. Tresckow seized opportunities, but left nothing to chance. He never decided to approach an officer without having observed him attentively. Rejecting any co-optation, he made up his own mind in each case.

At the end of 1942, our group included, in addition to Fabian von Schlabrendorff and myself, Carl-Friedrich von Berg-Schönefeld, Lieutenant-Colonels von Gersdorff and von Kleist – the latter known as Uncle Bernd[17] – and Major Pretzell. Major Alexander von Voss succeeded Schulze-Büttger. Pretzell was replaced by Hans-Ulrich von Oertzen, who incarnated the cavalry officer par excellence – cheerful, optimistic, elegant and refined. By definition the group could not remain stable, because all its members could be transferred to other posts or lose their lives in combat.

At that time there were at most thirty committed and resolute conspirators, that is, the largest body of opposing officers ever put together. None of us wanted to expand the group too much, out of concern for confidentiality, but also because we wished to spare lives by compromising as few people as possible. Our group could count on certain intermediaries. I had complete confidence in the aides-de-camp of the commanders-in-chief of the other two Army groups, for they were classmates and horsemen to boot – united by the cavalry's code of honour. With the marshal's authorization, I used the pretext of regular mail delivery to visit the other armies. Completely illegally, I exchanged maps of the front with my counterparts. Each of the conspirators put into action his own network that had been constituted before the war and usually consisted of classmates. Schlabrendorff played a crucial role in the organization of the Berlin network, which was composed of the former head of staff Beck, Hans Oster and General Olbricht. A trip by Tresckow to the capital would have looked suspicious, whereas the comings and goings of his orderly passed unnoticed.

My participation was valuable for the conspirators. Before the war, I had received, in Höxter's infantry regiment, a kind of training normally reserved for military engineers: how to use explosives. I kept a stock of different kinds of explosives of foreign origin. As a rule, explosives were rare, dangerous and kept under tight control. Precise records of all movements of stocks were kept. It was impossible, even for high officers in the Wehrmacht, and even within German territory, to divert significant quantities of explosives. I, however, was able to procure more or less anything I wanted. I therefore became the conspiracy's chief explosives expert, as it were. When our regiment was set up in April 1943, Stieff had designated it as an experimental unit (*Versuchstruppenteil*), and this provided me with an official justification for my tests, which allowed me to determine that English explosives were the most effective, particularly their detonators.

Nothing would be more incorrect than to imagine that we were a little group of conspirators entirely absorbed in our cause, spending whole nights consulting in a smoke-

filled room, remaking the world and planning assass-
inations. For our meetings, we took advantage of the
changing of the guard between day service and night
duty. The latter was assigned to officers ranking below
captain, and there were not enough of them to go around;
I often spontaneously volunteered. This gave me a
pretext for going to Tresckow's bunker. The night duty
began at 11 p.m., but Tresckow went to bed late, after a
ritual chess game that provided an opportunity to discuss
his projects with his circle of close associates. The meetings didn't last long; we didn't want to attract attention.
We were accustomed to concise orders, exact communications, and we seldom engaged in chatting or collective
reflection. At first, nonetheless, we discussed at great
length the legitimacy of our act and the justification for
murder – for an assassination, even of a tyrant, remains a
murder. Then we came to the practical aspects. Without
being directive, Tresckow was full of ideas, and his obser-
vations, which were always correct, were naturally
accepted by his comrades. However, he never spoke as a
superior officer, but always as a friend, with a paternal
gentleness that led us to share his convictions. We would
have liked to have him as a simple company captain. For
Tresckow we were less a closed group of impassioned
conspirators than a breeding ground for men ready to
sacrifice their lives, to act at the least signal, to execute
his plans without fail. Confidence and total availability
were our watchwords.

Tresckow was also looking for cover in the military
hierarchy. To be sure, the putsch would not come from
the generals, but Tresckow wanted at least to be sure that

they would keep quiet and wish him well. At the end of 1942, he tried to approach Marshal von Kluge through the intermediary of Carl-Friedrich von Berg-Schönefeld, the second-in-command of the intelligence services. While they were both out wolf-hunting, the lieutenant drew the marshal aside and surprised him by asking how he felt about Hitler. After having sounded the terrain, he asked what his reaction would be in the event that Hitler was physically eliminated. Their conversation stopped at that point; the lieutenant reported to Tresckow, who went to see the marshal the next day to inform him of his plans. Kluge exclaimed, 'Count on me!' He subsequently limited himself to an attitude of benevolent neutrality, and that was still enough to cost him his life.

The true motivations of the officers engaged in the enterprise are still the subject of lively controversy in Germany. We are said to have wanted to preserve our conquests at any price by concluding a separate peace with the Americans and the British that would make it possible to impose harsher conditions on the Soviets by shifting the war effort totally to them. We are supposed to have wanted to reestablish Germany's 1914 borders. I categorically deny that claim. The information we had left no doubt about the Allies' firm intentions; they would liquidate all the Reich's possessions outside the 1938 borders. With the United States' entry into the war, one didn't need to be a great strategist to see that such a vast economic power, spared fighting on its own soil, heavily tilted the scales in favour of our adversaries. The war was obviously lost, and none of the belligerents had an interest in making a separate peace with Germany. The Casablanca conference in January 1943 had, moreover, required Germany to surrender unconditionally. Finally, Hans Oster, whose counter-espionage services were the crossroads for the various conspiracies, informed us of discussions regarding the fate to be reserved for German territories that testified to the degree of solidarity among the Allies. For us, it was thus a question of putting an end to the hostilities and saving as many human lives as possible. Nothing more.

I recall a conversation that I had with Tresckow and Schulze-Büttger in early 1943. When I asked in a loud voice whether it was still worthwhile, given the military situation, to pursue our assassination plans, Tresckow gravely remarked: 'Gentlemen, every day we are assassinating nearly 16,000 additional victims. We have no choice.'

WHEN HORSES MAKE MEETINGS EASIER
(1943)

The German army had never ceased to use horses in support of the artillery, to substitute for failing machinery on the Russian front, and to aid bogged-down supply columns. Mobile and resilient, horses were often more reliable than machines.

Despite the exhaustion produced by the long marches we had made since summer, horses continued to render numerous services. The animals provided for the mounted cavalry could, at a trot, advance at 16 kilometres an hour, and draught horses at 13 kilometres an hour. The cold did not take them by surprise. Whereas the men tried to pad their thin uniforms with paper and rags, the horses' hair had thickened by itself, becoming almost like fur, to our great astonishment. When hay and oats began to run short on the immense, snowy plains the horses reacted by tearing off the tenderest branches of the pine trees. They even chewed on the edges of the cottages' thatched roofs when they could reach them. Finally they formed the habit of sucking icicles to get water. Their adaptability was phenomenal.

For the cavalrymen, horses were a kind of home. Our mounts carried our personal effects (clothing and other articles, toiletries) and the tents – each horseman carried a quarter of the latter. And what tender caresses the men and their animals exchanged when they saw each other again after a battle! Obviously, among horsemen, we were linked by camaraderie, mutual aid, and the certainty that even if they remained silent, your fellows understood and supported you. But the animals, their hair, their moist muzzles, their shivers paradoxically provided us with a physical intimacy, a warmth, that we could not allow ourselves even among our best comrades. In the extreme severity of war, the men confided in their horses, depended on them. The horse, for its part, was incapable of surviving without its master's care. And in the end it is hard to say which was the more useful to the other, the horseman or the mount.

For a long time my brother Georg had been thinking about how to mobilize the tactical potential of the cavalry. On this immense front, it was not firepower and the abundance of materiel alone that would decide the outcome of the fighting. Furthermore, from this point of view, the German army did not have the advantage. With an industrial base damaged by the depression and now handicapped by air raids, it would never be able to produce as many artillery shells and munitions as it did in 1917. It would never succeed in challenging the superiority of the enemy since the United States had begun providing them with armaments. Nor would human resources be able to turn the war around. In this fifth year of the war, the age group born between 1915 and 1925 had already been decimated. It would be necessary to call upon younger and younger recruits, hastily trained. The rotation of troops was particularly tragic in the infantry. To sow disorder among the adversary, close the breaches, and cover our retreat, what we needed was mobility, an ability to react, and a more economical use of materiel. In apparently hopeless situations, such as Christmas 1941, Georg's cavalrymen had played a decisive role and made it possible to avoid disaster by galloping toward the rear to set up a line of defence, and by galloping forward to sow chaos among the enemy.

My brother had two models. With his open-minded intelligence and his habit of judging solely on merit, he had chosen his models among the enemy. In the end, Georg didn't have any enemies, only adversaries: he never expressed either hatred or scorn in speaking of the Russians. His first model was Major-General Dovator, the commandant of the Red Army's Third Cavalry Corps, which had succeeded in penetrating the German front line on 13 December 1941 and cut off German communications and supply convoys. His enthusiasm didn't give Dovator much chance of survival: he was killed a few days later, at the age of thirty-seven. Georg's second model was General Belov, who survived the war. In November 1941, while he was commanding the Soviet Second Cavalry Corps supported by a tank division, Belov had already routed and repelled several Wehrmacht divisions. In early 1942, with incredible boldness he had pierced the German front line at Dorogobush, penetrated deeply behind the lines, hooked up with the partisans, and held on until the end of March in a situation where he was completely surrounded.

For our cavalrymen scattered over different divisions, the constitution of a specialized regiment was a question of survival. Georg had long meditated on all this while he was in Romania. On 26 December 1942, after a short leave in Heimerzheim, he travelled into the heart of Russia, not without stopping to see his comrades in the old 6th Battalion squadron. Of its officers, the only survivor was Wilhelm König, whom his colleagues had for years called only by his nickname, 'King'. Georg was given an enthusiastic welcome by his former sub-ordinates.[18] I had done everything I could to make his journey easier and, since the road to Rshew passed not far from Smolensk, where the Army Group Centre had its headquarters, I set up an interview for him with Marshal von Kluge on 8 January 1943. With the capacity for conviction that was peculiar to him, Georg explained to the commander-in-chief the tactical advantages of the cavalry: its mobility, its swiftness, its indifference to weather conditions, and its ability to harass the enemy, despite its small numbers and its modest firepower. Kluge had met my brother before the war, when he was in charge of the Westphalian military region. He had heard about Georg's exploits in France and his spotless military career. He listened in silence. The next day – having slept on it – the marshal said that he had been convinced by my brother's demonstration, and was prepared to try out the idea. 'Go and work out all the details with Tresckow,' he advised Georg.

I organized the meeting. Georg and Tresckow were leaders of men, true tacticians. They were able to judge and assess each other in a few moments; their discussion was brief. In a letter to Georg on 27 July, Tresckow summed up their meeting and their intermittent contacts over the next six months: 'We have seen each other only a few times, but I think these brief moments are enough for us to know what we are doing together. I will always be loyal to you, and I would be grateful for your loyalty in return. And now, keep it under your hat!'

The two men had resolved to set up an autonomous cavalry force that would serve not only military ends but might also, under Georg's command, be used in the framework of a coup d'etat. This force completed Tresckow's arrangements for the overthrow of the regime: in addition to Kluge's approval and a network of officers in whom he could have confidence, he could now count on operational mobile units commanded by people loyal to him. A great many practical details remained to be dealt with. A few weeks earlier, Colonel Helmut Stieff, another member of our network, had been appointed head of the Army General Staff's 'Organization Department', and he shared Tresckow's views regarding the double function of the cavalrymen. Less than a week after his meeting with Georg, Tresckow received Stieff's instructions. On 14 January, he could order the immediate regrouping, under Georg's command, of the vestiges of the main cavalry units.

The involvement of his cavalry unit in the group's projects did not remain secret. Franz von Papen, who was then the German ambassador in Ankara, writes in his memoirs that in April 1943 he had a confidential discussion with Count von Helldorf, the Berlin police superintendent, and Gottfried von Bismarck, the governor of Potsdam. The latter told him about plots against Hitler in which the cavalry regiment led by Georg von

Boeselager, who was mentioned by name, was to capture the head of state and the principal leaders of the Nazi party. This description, though somewhat deformed by rumour, shows what a dangerous position my brother and I found ourselves in. Fortunately, these three high officials were playing a double game and took care not to mention this information to the Reich's dreaded state security police.

Outside these authorized circles, the news about the establishment of a cavalry group spread like wildfire within the little world of the cavalry. On 25 January, König and his men had reached Smolensk. Soon thereafter – having been brought into the operation a few weeks later – I left the marshal's service to join them. Georg worked hard to bring in all the usable cavalry squadrons, to provide them with the proper number of horses again, to set up sufficient artillery cover, to provide the units with communications equipment, to recreate support functions from the ground up, and to recruit a sufficient number of veterinarians, because one of his major concerns was to ensure that the horses would be well cared for. When spring came, the mares gave birth to seventy colts, which were sent, after a few weeks of being nursed by their mothers, to East Prussia. The horses consumed a large quantity of fodder, which was for the most part imported from Germany. A normal-sized horse needs five kilograms of straw per day, and the same amounts of hay and oats. We had to procure this feed in sufficient quantities, and especially to get ready for winter. So we constructed a wooden haypress that allowed us to make rectangular bales that would be stored for the cold season. Georg was willing to deal with every detail. He had as much confidence in the marshal as I did, but nothing was simple. He wrote, telephoned, inspected, located things, visited the herds of horses; he observed, judged, weighed. He pestered Berlin with multiple requests, hoping to wear the officials down. The Army General Staff looked with favour on his projects, and Georg had a good contact in Major von Amsberg, the officer charged with supervising the cavalry, whom he had met on the Orient Express the preceding summer on his way to Romania.

Absorbed by his incessant activity, Georg almost forgot to eat and drink. A few eggs, a quart of coffee, or cup of mocca seemed to be enough for him. He slept only five hours a night. He didn't even have time to ride his five horses every day; he had entrusted their dressage to Fritz Thiedemann. The only relaxation he allowed himself was to go hunting at dawn, often alone with his dog. Sometimes ranging over the steppe or the forests, sometimes going deep into the marshes, he rediscovered the joys of his youth, hiding in the bushes to look for game. A rabbit or a fox in his gamebag, he came back a few hours later, just as the camp was waking up. His mind clear, he gave his orders and the day began.

According to Tresckow's instructions, the cavalry group was supposed to have twenty-eight officers, 160 non-commissioned officers, 920 troopers, and a little more than a thousand horses. By the end of February, 350 Cossacks joined the group; their integration was handled by Captain von der Schulenburg. The cavalry group, called the Boeselager Reiterverband, was then composed of four cavalry squadrons, a mortar battery, an intelligence detachment and an artillery squadron. On 6 April, the group was transformed into a genuine regiment composed of two battalions. The first was commanded by Captain Walther Schmidt-Salzmann, and I took command of the second.

THE THREE FAILED ATTEMPTS IN MARCH 1943

Only a handful of officers were in contact with the Führer. Among them were his personal aide-de-camp, Rudolph Schmundt, a classmate of Tresckow's, and, of course, the marshals. But an officer below the rank of general had very few opportunities to approach the dictator and thus to assassinate him. Before any meeting, moreover, one had to remove one's belt and one's personal weapon. Thus Tresckow thought that it would be much easier to eliminate Hitler when he came to visit the Russian front than to seek him out in his impregnable Wolf's Lair (*Wolfsschanze*), or even on German territory. The Army Group Centre was only one of the three armies on the Eastern Front. Moreover, the Führer had a temporary headquarters on the Russian Front and hardly moved around among the troops at all. Tresckow nonetheless succeeded in drawing Hitler into a trap. Through the intermediary of Schmundt, he let it be known that Kluge was violently opposed to launching operation 'Citadel'. To allay the marshal's annoyance, Hitler had to visit the front in order to restore confidence, if not harmony. The plea produced its effect. The Führer was asked to cajole the marshal, and he was tempted by the amusing prospect of manipulating and converting his detractor. It remained only to set a date for the visit.

We were not sure whether to use a firearm or explosives in making our attempt on the Führer's life. The choice of a bomb limited the opportunities to act, and it would cause a larger number of casualties not only outside Hitler's immediate entourage, but also among the conspirators themselves. Thus we decided to use a pistol, without, however, excluding the use of explosives in the event of failure. The solution we adopted did not, for all that, guarantee certain success. Through Schmundt, Tresckow had learned that the dictator wore a thin bullet-proof vest under his uniform. In addition, Baron von Gersdorff had observed that the Führer's cap was lined with metal. In short, although Hitler didn't wear armour, the assassin would have to aim carefully at some unprotected part of his body. We were not sufficiently well informed to be sure that the shot would kill him. Thus we arrived at the conclusion that it would be necessary to shoot him in the face.

We were actively preparing ourselves, working out scenarios, practising our aim. However, we had to decide who was going to pull the trigger. Shooting somebody in the back already demands a great deal of sangfroid, and shooting him from the front is still more difficult. But shooting someone in the face is something else again. Georg saw Tresckow daily in order to ensure that his cavalry group would have priority. One day Tresckow suddenly asked him directly whether he was prepared to assassinate the man who had solemnly decorated him a year earlier. My brother was a man of resolute temperament, and hunting had made him a good shot.

Tresckow had decided that he wouldn't get rattled. Georg reflected for a moment, and then conceded that he couldn't guarantee that he could hit the target. He was not afraid for his life, though a one-man assassination attempt would expose the shooter to the bodyguards' fire. He was not afraid of being weak. He was afraid that he might be too nervous to aim correctly.

He therefore agreed, but only on the condition that he should not be alone. There were nine conspirators in all, four from the staff and five from the cavalry unit being formed. Among the former were Captain Schmidt-Salzmann and myself. I had delayed for a month the assumption of my command, which was initially scheduled for 1 March 1943, so as to be able to devote myself more fully to preparing for the assassination attempt. The scenario was the following: once Hitler had come into the mess hall and sat down to eat lunch, Georg was to stand up, count 'one, two', and then the rest of us would also stand up and fire. There would probably be a few bodyguards present, but they would be on the sides of the room, because they were not seated at the main tables. Obviously, we were expecting them to react, but we were counting on the confusion created by the shooting to make their reaction ineffective. It was as simple as that. Everyone knew exactly his position and his role. It was important that there be several shooters, in case an unforeseen obstacle intercepted one of the bullets. We had planned a backup solution in the event that the lunch was cancelled at the last minute, Hitler not being fond of banquets.

If this scenario could not be carried out, Wilhelm

König's cavalry squadron was to intercept the Führer while he was passing through the forest and hand him over to an improvised military tribunal, which would sentence him to a firing squad. Finally, as a last resort, Schlabrendorff had proposed putting explosives in the Führer's plane.

It remained to tell Kluge about our preparations. He knew what his operations officer was doing and secretly shielded him. His tacit approval was limited only by his legendary intelligence and prudence – he had been nicknamed 'Gunther the Crafty'. To this sixty-year-old Prussian imbued by tradition, assassinating Hitler while he was eating lunch seemed a little cowardly on the part of German officers. He had another reservation: the German people would not understand the murder of a man who was still perceived as an energetic war leader and the last rampart against humiliating defeat. Hence when I asked him about it, the field marshal did not answer me. Instead, he gestured with his chin in such a way as to signify: 'Do it at your own risk ... I won't denounce you.'

On 7 March, Dohnanyi, Hans Oster's assistant, came to the headquarters of Army Group Centre. Coded signals had been set up with him to launch the coup d'état in the event that the assassination succeeded. On 12 March 1943, the day before the Führer was to visit, we learned that Himmler would not be coming along on the trip. Kluge withdrew his approval at the last minute: to kill Hitler without seizing Himmler was to risk starting a civil war. The SS would take power as soon as the Führer was dead and would begin a merciless repression.

They would then have to be dislodged from supreme power as well. In short, Hitler's elimination, though possible, would not have strategic importance without the concomitant liquidation of the Reichsführer SS. The operation was cancelled, and we were overwhelmed by a feeling of disappointment proportional to our investment in the project.

The Führer's plane, a Wulf Condor that was flying in from Vinnytsia, landed at the aerodrome. The stairs were lowered, the door opened, and Hitler came down. Himmler was not there. The day was unbearable. At every stage of the visit, we were mentally following the development of the scenario we had so long planned, timed and prepared. Hitler and Kluge were meeting in the conference room; I can still see the Führer's personal doctor, Professor Theo Morell, snoring in the waiting room, his mouth open, insolent and tranquil while we cooled our heels. During the lunch, we had to put up with Hitler's good humour; he was glad to be in contact with real soldiers. The Führer had brought along his personal cook and the doctor assigned to taste his food. Hunched over his plate, his elbows on the table, raising his head only to swallow a mouthful of wine, he was a despicable sight.

We obeyed the marshal's interdiction. But Tresckow and Schlabrendorff had planned something else. Such a fine opportunity could not be missed. Hitler was not to end the day alive. Schlabrendorff, as a simple reserve officer, felt less bound by the obligation to obey incumbent on the soldier. During lunch Tresckow had ascertained that his tablemate, Colonel Brandt, was going to be in the Führer's plane on the way back. On the pretext of surprising Helmut Stieff, Schlabrendorff gave Brandt two bottles of French cognac in a wooden case. Gifts of wine and spirits were frequently made among military men, and the sentry in charge of security for the plane was easily taken in by Schlabrendorff's ruse. It was in reality a case of explosives, whose preparation had cost me several nights' work. The detonator, which Schlabrendorff had activated, was timed to explode the bomb in mid-flight, somewhere near Minsk.

Our stupefaction was boundless when we learned that evening that the Führer's plane had landed safely in Rastenburg, in East Prussia, after an uneventful flight. We were crushed. For Fabian von Schlabrendorff, the news was still more threatening. However, it was not yet time for lamentations. We had to act quickly, but not so hastily that we would awaken suspicion. Hence we could not arrange to take a special plane. The next day at dawn, Schlabrendorff left in a regularly scheduled mail plane. Two hours later, he was at the aerodrome where the Führer had landed. Retaining his sangfroid, he found Brandt, recovered his case of cognac, and exchanged real wine bottles for the explosives. On examination, it turned out that the detonator had not functioned properly. The problem had probably been caused by the extremely low temperature in the plane's baggage compartment.

The following week, in Berlin, Gersdorff was supposed to show the Führer some of the spoils taken from the Soviets. He was to accompany General Model. Tresckow had managed at the last minute to send this pro-Nazi general instead of Kluge, whom he wanted to be available in the event that the assassination attempt succeeded. This 20 March was 'Heroes' Day', dedicated to the memory of the hundreds of thousands of soldiers who had already fallen at the front. Goebbels and Göring were also to be present. Another unhoped-for opportunity. Gersdorff was supposed to sacrifice himself in this attempt. Our common desire to eliminate the Führer was such that Gersdorff hadn't hesitated for a moment when Tresckow suggested the idea to him. A few moments after the Führer entered the arsenal, he activated the time-bomb attached to his belt. Unfortunately, Hitler was in a hurry, and passed through the exposition at a run, without listening to any of the explanations and without pausing before the display cases, despite Göring's urging. Left alone, Gersdorff had time to rush to the lavatory, smash the detonator, and flush it down the toilet. He had saved his life. But Hitler was still alive.

These two failures, which occurred a week apart, were not enough to destroy our morale. We knew we could count on each other; that was what was important. But looking back, I have to admit that Kluge was right. In March 1943, our conspiracy was not yet mature enough to be effective. The simple physical elimination of the Führer would not have solved anything unless it was combined with a well-planned coup d'état. We would only have paved the way for another despot, who might have been still more bloodthirsty. It was in fact highly unlikely that the elite anti-Nazi elements would agree to expose themselves in order to organize an immediate and coordinated reaction.

STOPPING THE BARBARIANS

When the fighting on the Eastern Front began, German officers felt that they represented civilization in a battle against a barbarous nation. What is barbarism? First of all, it is a complete disrespect for the rights of individuals, brutality in human relationships, savagery in the actions of everyday life, and finally indifference to all the achievements in culture and comfort, to everything that centuries of labour and the progress of the human spirit have produced that is beautiful. These communists whose agents shot down without hesitation soldiers who had retreated, these officers without conscience who, in order to exhaust German munitions, sent ragtag groups of women, old men and children gathered together in haste towards us to be mown down by our machine guns; these enemies who systematically killed the wounded, put out the eyes of their prisoners, and didn't deign to bury their own dead – they all seemed barbarians to us. We had heard many stories of this kind, and we had seen many macabre proofs that they were true. But for months we had known that the Russians had no monopoly on barbarism: bestiality had taken hold of the SS and their auxiliaries, and even regular soldiers sometimes acted with pointless cruelty. We had not only to prevent the

Russian steamroller from crushing Eastern Europe, but also to limit the SS's capacity for destruction. This conviction, at first vaguely felt, was quickly confirmed for me.

In early spring 1943, when I had just taken command of my battalion, Bettermann, who commanded the artillery group, asked to speak to me privately. He seemed very upset. For two days, on his way back from leave, he had travelled in the same railway car with SS-men and men from the Sicherheitsdienst (SD). In the midst of this group, he had had to put up with their endless conversations. The SS-men were loudly bragging about having liquidated, in Army Group South's sector, no less than 250,000 Jews. Drunk on brandy and the liquor loosening their tongues, they took pleasure in recounting the massacres, mixing cruel and obscene details. Though he turned away in disgust, my artillery man still heard that they were soon to move into Army Group Centre's sector to pursue their work there.

I didn't hesitate for a second; I called Georg on the phone: 'I have to see Kluge, immediately!'

'What's wrong?' Georg asked, astonished by my agitation.

'Major, I'll tell you later. Nothing to do with the regiment!'

'All right, go ahead,' Georg said, hanging up; he had understood the gravity of the situation by my intonation and the official formula I'd used.

Less than an hour later, I was at headquarters. The marshal saw me immediately, and took what I said very seriously. 'We absolutely have to prevent such a catastrophe. Go see Tresckow and take care of it.'

Faithful to his reputation, Tresckow provided the solution to a problem that appeared insoluble. It was impossible to prevent the Sicherheitsdienst from coming in, or to prevent its members from committing atrocities. The ground had to be cut out from under them, they had to be deprived of the means of conducting roundups. Tresckow ordered all local commandants to prohibit any assembly of citizens within their areas. If they could not gather their victims together before putting them into the trucks, the SS would be seriously hindered. In fact, the SD's anti-Semitic atrocities were more limited in this zone than in others on the Eastern Front, and especially in Ukraine. I was able to confirm this when visiting the Yad Vashem memorial in Jerusalem a few years ago.

Cavalrymen in Torment

During a lecture I gave in Paris in January 2004 before a group of secondary school students, along with other members of the German and French resistance, a young man asked me: 'But why, after all, didn't you organize other conspiracies? Why didn't you try again and again?'

'It was wartime!' I replied. 'Our primary role, as officers, was to make sure our men survived and returned home.'

It seems to me important to make this point. It is true that our objective was to eliminate the Führer and to overthrow the regime. We were doing our duty, fulfilling our ultimate obligation. But we also had an immediate operational assignment, a responsibility toward the men whom we commanded that could not be evaded. The Eastern Front took virtually all our energy, our concentration, and our physical and psychological capacities. The dates planned for assassination attempts were intertwined with the requirements of the operational calendar. That is why, the day before the Führer visited our headquarters in March 1943, Georg and his men had been far more absorbed in an engagement with guerrilla forces than with the material preparation for the assassination.

In May, the cavalry group was still heavily involved in fighting with the partisans around Staiki, between Vitebsk and Orsha. During the retreat, it was one of the few units that remained mobile, while the trucks were floundering in the melted snow, their advance halted by streams that had turned into torrents. Then the regiment was given a supplementary battalion commanded by Captain von Bassewitz. Fortunately, the operational necessities left us a few moments of relaxation. In June, for example, we organized an equestrian tournament and a Roman chariot race – with drivers wearing togas ...

When we had nothing else to do, we performed intensive training exercises in 'dismounting to fight' (*Absitzen zum Kampf*). The horses had long since become accustomed to the din of firing, the sound of explosions, and the shouts of the combatants, and they showed an amazing placidity. But they remained vulnerable to fire. In each battle, the cavalry had to be ready to dismount at short notice, leaving their animals without brusqueness and handing them over to one of their comrades who was assigned to take them a few hundred paces towards the rear. The men responsible for this manoeuvre, who remained in the saddle, had to be able to hold the bridle of one horse in his right hand and hold the reins of two more in his left. They departed at a trot, under the direction of an experienced adjutant, to wait out the fighting in the shelter of a forest or behind a hill. The little group of horses was then brought back to the combatants, sometimes guided by radio when the circumstances of the battle had forced the unit to move. These manoeuvres had to be carried out in a few minutes at most. The quality of the training explains why the loss of mounts was minimal – so much so that in 1945 I was able to return home with Moritz and Oter, the horses that had been with me since 1939.

Soon, however, the fighting became more serious. On 5 July 1943, Hitler launched operation 'Citadel', which was supposed to reduce or even annihilate the formidable offensive potential the enemy had assembled in the Kursk salient, an area between Army Group Centre and Army Group South. The cavalry regiment was to play a decisive role. A true 'visiting fireman', as Marshal von Kluge wished it to be, the regiment's mission was to be continually on the move to put out fires.

On 12 July 1943, eighty Soviet rifle divisions, supported by air cover and 3,500 tanks, attacked from the west and the north the Orel-Briansk panhandle, where large numbers of German troops had been concentrated for an attack on the Kursk salient, farther to the south. Two hundred kilometres south-west of Moscow, the Orel region was an indentation penetrating into Russian territory, and was symmetrical to the Kursk salient which bulged into the positions held by the Wehrmacht.

Tresckow foresaw that we would be in danger of being surrounded if the Red Army succeeded in seizing the Orel-Karachev-Briansk rail line. He decided to send one of our battalions to the sector of Tereben, a large village north-east of Karachev. The infantry's ability to resist was exhausted there, and the line of defence was in the process of collapsing. Georg designated me for the operation. We put our 600 men on a train camouflaged with whole birch trees, along with 62 light machine guns,

12 heavy machine guns, an anti-tank gun and an anti-aircraft gun.

Going ahead of our troops, Georg and I arrived at the command post in Tereben during the night of 17 July. We found it in total confusion. Two commandants were arguing over who was to take the initiative. Georg reconciled them by depriving both of any authority over their seven battalions. Then gunshots rang out north of the village. The troops, panicked, began running down the streets. Georg, his pistol in his hand, worked his way up the human stream, managed to turn the movement around and to rally the defenders. The men recovered their courage, but the adversary's numerical superiority was incontestable. To hold Tereben, we had to temporarily abandon the defence of the village of Kudrjavez, four kilometres to the south-east. The next day, however, Georg was ordered to retake this village. We had to catch the enemy by surprise. I left with my men at 8 a.m. on 20 July, went around the village on the west side, continued a few kilometres further south, and then, suddenly changing direction, headed north and penetrated enemy territory, destroying on the way a Russian supply column. Georg, who had taken up a position north of the village, guided our movements by radio. In two hours, the village had been retaken along with important booty, especially intelligence material. Our casualties included three dead and twenty-one wounded. The respite was short.

At dawn on 23 July, the enemy resumed the offensive. Seven Russian rifle regiments attacked the defence line, which had been hastily set up and was lightly manned.

Georg used his units as emergency reinforcements. As soon as our infantrymen weakened at a point, he brought in one or two detachments of forty cavalrymen, who dispersed the Russian infantry, re-established the line, and then went to deal with another hot spot. Everything would no doubt have collapsed had it not been for Georg, who was fighting amidst his troops.

The 3rd Cavalry Squadron found itself in the worst difficulties. It had lost contact with the troops on its left and right. Reduced in half an hour to 110 men, it thought it was already doomed to be completely wiped out. Then Georg suddenly emerged from thicket, accompanied by his driver. Wearing his forage cap while bullets whistled around his ears and armed only with a pistol stuck into his belt and a stick in his hand, he went to join the head of the squadron. With total self-control, he asked for an update on the situation, as if the drama being played out all around him were only a training manoeuvre. The men saw him, and his obvious assurance was enough to reinvigorate them. Like a teacher, Georg then asked: 'All right, now, what would you do? Would you make a frontal attack? Or would you prefer to infiltrate laterally between the two enemy regiments?' The leader of the squadron opted for a frontal advance. Georg took a few moments to think: 'Fine, stay here, and don't give up an inch of terrain, re-establish connection with the unit on your left, and I'll take care of the rest.' Thirty minutes later, with the squadron placed under his direct command, he attacked the enemy regiment's flank, and the latter began to retreat. Georg immediately returned to the 3rd Squadron and asked that it resume a total offensive in coordination with the lateral attack. The operation worked perfectly. The Russians were driven back. But we had gained only a few hours, because the enemy's firepower was overwhelming. Soon Tereben was in flames. Our three battalions were much diminished. Two battalions were still more or less able to fight, but exhausted by the incessant battles of the preceding days, they would not hold out for long. The cavalrymen, who were still operational, saw the number of their able-bodied troops cut in half.

By about 4 p.m. on 24 July, we had to face facts and give up Tereben and Kudrjavez. The new objective was the bridge over the Resseta, a little to the west. At the risk of cutting off their own retreat, Georg's men blew up the bridge at 6 p.m. The remaining troops were supposed to move about fifteen kilometres to the south-west along the river, while at the same time protecting the rail line; the Russians pursuing them were threatening to pass them by on the left flank. Between the adversary and the German units there was a marshy area. Here and there little thickets grew on the spongy soil. The rest was a broad marsh, sometimes a metre deep, infested with mosquitoes and leeches. On 27 July, we were ordered to attack. In two hours of fighting that was fierce but prudently conducted, we routed the enemy battalion, capturing dozens of Russian soldiers caught in the watery trap.

By 29 July, the situation had been stabilized. We were relieved by two neighbouring divisions. Georg and I remained in reserve in the sector until 8 August. These two weeks of intense fighting had resulted in a limited number of losses to the 1st Boeselager Battalion: 7 per cent dead, 29 per cent wounded.

During the summer, our regiment's various battalions were successively mobilized for service in several hot spots around Smolensk. The scenario was always the same: the enemy's numerical superiority, penetrations that sowed panic in our ranks, the rapid intervention of the cavalry, creating a temporary stabilization, the evacuation of what could be evacuated, and then, under assault by further waves of attackers, an orderly retreat of our units. The cavalrymen, in short, provided for an organized management of the inevitable retreat.

In mid-September, Kluge succeeded in convincing Hitler to abandon Smolensk. The Army Group Centre retreated on a part of the front called the 'Panther Line', which stretched from Vitebsk in the north to Gomel in the south. On 25 September, the marshal ordered Georg to concentrate his troops south-east of Orsha; they were to be put at the disposition of the Fourth Army. Our regiment covered the 126 kilometres in thirty-six hours and reached the point indicated on 27 September at 8 a.m. We had to go immediately on the attack. For the first time, we took as part of our booty American radio equipment, tangible proof of deliveries from the United States to their Soviet ally. In early October, its mission accomplished, the regiment moved back to the north, under torrential rains.

But the regiment had to prepare itself for graver ordeals. Towards mid October, the Russians broke the Panther Line at several points. On the assumption that such a break might take place, the line had been backed up by an East Panther Line and a line of retreat, the West Panther Line, separated by a few kilometres. One day, a reconnaissance patrol that I had sent into this insecure area came under enemy fire. It took refuge in a forest and wandered about for a whole day in the marshy undergrowth, where the horses sank in up to their bellies. Sandbanks with pines on them emerged here and there from the watery expanse. The patrol bivouacked on one of these sandbanks, curled up on a few square metres like a hedgehog in a defensive position. The men ended up giving their own bread ration to the exhausted horses, for whom the birch branches they were offered were not enough. The next day, avoiding the enemy, the patrol managed to rejoin the battalion. How relieved I was to see these boys that I thought were lost! I handed out cognac liberally and gave each man twenty cigarettes – a luxury in those times of crisis.

Georg soon decided to use the battalion I commanded, because the 2nd Battalion had been overworked in the preceding weeks. My unit's strength had already been sharply diminished; I had only a third of my normal number of machine guns. So it was with nineteen light machine guns, four heavy machine guns and seven grenade-launchers that we took up, on 21 October, the position in Sapolje that had been assigned to us. The mission was simple but suicidal. We were supposed to retake part of the old East Panther Line that the Soviets had held comfortably for several days.

Georg went out alone in the early dawn to examine the terrain. He saw that the enemy, overwhelming two infantry companies, had made a breakthrough. Quickly

marshalling two detachments of cavalrymen on a reconnaissance mission that he had happened to run into, he
launched, in his own way, an improvised counter-attack.
The little group (fewer than seventy cavalrymen) headed
toward the Russians at a gallop. The soldiers then noticed
with terror that Georg was not armed. They offered him
a pistol, but he laughed and rode on. When the Russians
came into view, Georg separated his troops into two
detachments, which attacked the enemy on both flanks.
Taken by surprise, the Russians were routed in a few
minutes, leaving behind them forty prisoners and as
many dead. Without delay, our men galloped off to the
regiment's operations command post.

The next day, my men retook the village of Redki
without a fight. Then we were ordered to take a rise
somewhat to the south of the village, known as hill 208.
We approached it without difficulty. But we still had to
cross a natural glacis – 200 metres of open slope leading
to the summit. In briefing the troops, I had been clear:
'The quicker we carry out the assault, the few losses we'll
have.' I was not wrong. Mortar shells fell all around us.
We had to launch several attacks in order to take the hill,
with considerable losses, and ended up fighting hand to
hand. We achieved our objective in the afternoon, but
we already had thirty-two dead, which meant that we
had lost nearly 10 per cent of our troops. And we still
hadn't won, because less than a kilometre away the
Russian artillery, positioned on another hill, was able to
shell the one we had taken with such difficulty. The
Russians had long-range cannons, and their aim was
accurate. A whole group of my men was cut down, or

rather pulverized, as soon as it took up positions on the summit. We worked all night, restoring the trenches and re-supplying the 400 square metre area at the foot of the hill that separated the battalion from the next division. We also took advantage of the darkness to evacuate the dead and wounded, who had been loaded onto small carts.

At dawn, the Russians attacked. They had crept up to the foot of the hill, using the small bushes and depressions in the terrain as cover. They were thrown back twice. Here, the cavalrymen were fighting like infantry in trench warfare, using rifles and machine guns. When it got light, the Russian artillery resumed its intensive bombardment, concentrating its firepower on the summit of the hill. The exploding shells shredded the thin layer of grass on top of the hill, uncovering sandy, shifting soil. Dust blew in everywhere, jamming the last machine guns that had not been put out of commission by the Soviet artillery. I was wounded, but still remained on the battlefield for some time. By 10 o'clock, I was too weak and dizzy with pain to stay any longer, and had to be evacuated. By 11.30, the situation had become critical. The hill could no longer be held. Our losses were too great and the attacks were unrelenting, coming one wave after another. Several of the battalion's units had lost 95 per cent of their men, killed or wounded. The operational forces thrown into battle by the regimental commandant had been reduced to 120 men. At nightfall, the few dozen remaining able-bodied men were preparing to abandon the hill when Russian patrols attacked the lines, broke through the defences, and began to surround our troops. Pursuers and pursued were mixed up in the same chaotic race. Our men retreated as best they could towards the operations command post that had been set up in the village.

Georg was inside the command post. His second-in-command, Lieutenant Gigas, was struggling to establish a telephone connection with the divisional command post. 'Major,' he said, 'something is wrong on the main highway and hill 208, there's heavy fire and it's getting closer.' Georg didn't realize how great the threat was until Dr Keltsch, the 1st Battalion's doctor, suddenly burst into the shack. 'The Russians are here,' he cried breathlessly. Georg hurried outside and saw about sixty exhausted men grouped around the few armoured vehicles he had at his disposal in the Redki sector. Three tanks were quickly rounded up, along with two anti-aircraft guns. They were firing blindly into the dark. The Russians were coming down the slopes of the hill in successive waves and falling upon the remains of the battalion, protected by the darkness. 'Alert the engineering troops in Ssudilovitch', Georg shouted to Lieutenant Gigas, before collapsing; he had been hit by an enemy bullet. The staff's doctor, Dr Deecke, saw that Georg had a deep wound in his hip. My brother was evacuated. Gigas, whom Georg had put in command, had great difficulty in evacuating the men toward the West Panther Line. On the way, the group, already small, was attacked, leaving behind still more dead and once again overwhelmed by panic. The lieutenant managed to re-establish order in the ranks by pointing out that they were crossing a minefield with only a very narrow path that was safe.

At last they reached the longed-for German lines. The men collapsed with fatigue. Though in retreat, Lieutenant Gigas had retained his ability to make decisions. He sent a handful of soldiers back to Redki where the Russians were celebrating their rout of the Germans with heavy drinking. Without being noticed, the patrol managed to slip into the little house that had served as a command post. There it recovered maps, intelligence material and Georg's precious fur-lined coat, and then returned to our lines safe and sound.

On 28 October, the remains of the regiment were withdrawn from the Panther Line and left the Fourth Army. For two months, the regiment rebuilt its strength, trained recruits, transformed hundreds of infantry men into cavalrymen, and incorporated new officers.

Georg and I, who had been wounded a few hours apart, were both taken to the military hospital in Minsk. We were soon joined there by Marshal von Kluge. Seriously injured in a car accident – partisans had thrown a milk can at his windshield – he had given up command of the Army Group Centre. Less than a month later, I was able to resume command of my battalion. Georg's wound, which was more problematic, forced him to do desk work until the end of December. He continued to direct operations from a distance. He went to great lengths to obtain authorization to equip his men with 43/1 machine guns, which were very easy to handle and well adapted to the Russian context. In pursuing this project he was running counter to the views of Hitler's entourage, which feared that an excessive diversification of armaments would have deleterious effects on production lines. He finally got what he wanted; the Ministry of Armament surreptitiously encouraged experimentation with new equipment, and almost 2,000 new weapons were delivered in early 1944.

Despite the soldiers' bravery, the sacrifice of whole units, and the technical quality of the command, the Wehrmacht could no longer stand up to an enemy that was constantly growing in numbers and increasingly well-equipped. According to Kluge's analysis, the Army Group Centre needed more than 200,000 additional men. Each division had to hold a sector 20 to 30 kilometres long, and the front lines had become too porous to allow the cavalry to fill the gaps. The Eastern Front was disintegrating.

THE VALISE FULL OF EXPLOSIVES

In the early autumn of 1943, Georg ordered me to take some explosives to General Stieff. In concert with Tresckow, then on leave in Berlin, he had started looking again for practical ways to carry out operation 'Valkyrie', from a bomb attack to a coup d'état. It was not a question of an isolated assassination, but rather of beginning a complete overthrow of the regime.

As the regiment's bomb expert, I had access to explosives in reasonable quantities, and had no difficulty removing some from our stocks. I took a regularly scheduled flight to the Army's headquarters in the Mauerwald camp near Lötzen, 15 kilometres from the Führer's Wolfsschanze. In my leather valise, I carried explosives and detonators. The explosives were in the form of twenty bricks sheathed in aluminium.

The lingering effects of my wounds still made me limp, and it was therefore agreed that a car would be waiting to take me to Stieff. When I got to the aerodrome however, there was no one there to meet me, and I tried to limp along carrying my heavy load. I had to ward off a zealous non-commissioned officer who was passing through and offered me his help. Finally, the car turned up and took me to Helmut Stieff. The general was in a conference, and I had to wait. Impatient, nervous and clinging to my valise, I slipped into the staff's cinema, which was open day and night. The darkness provided a little tranquillity, but I couldn't pay the slightest bit of attention to the comedy that was being shown – *Das Bad auf der Tenne* ('Swimming in the Thames'). Spectators were coming and going as they they went on and off duty. I gripped my valise with both hands, holding it between my legs and taking care that no one tripped over it. Finally someone came to get me. Stieff asked that he not be disturbed for any reason, and we locked ourselves into a windowless archive room. In a few minutes, I handed over the explosives, explained how to use them, took my leave, and returned by the same route.

It was only after the war that I found out what happened to my valise. In November, Stieff went on leave and entrusted the explosives to Lieutenant Herwarth von Bitterfeld,[19] General Köstring's second-in-command, who was in charge of the troops on the Eastern Front. At that time, Herwarth and his boss lived in a barracks called the *Jägerhöhe*, near Army headquarters. Their rooms were located opposite each other on the same hallway. German women from the Banat region cleaned the rooms every other day, one side of the hallway and then the other. Herwarth had hidden the precious valise under his bed. When his room was to be cleaned, he slipped it under the general's bed, across the hall, and took it back the same evening. He'd told Köstring what Stieff had told him: 'Don't look in the valise, its contents are too hot for you!' Thus for several months the valise travelled back and forth between the two rooms.

In early summer 1944, Stieff recovered the valise and gave it to Claus von Stauffenberg.[20] What happened next is well known.

Obligatory Inactivity

From November 1943 to March 1944, Georg and I spent more time in military hospitals than on the battlefield. My brother's condition continually deteriorated. He had returned to his troops shortly before Christmas, 1943. But his immune system had been weakened by overwork and excessive fatigue, and he really needed to remain completely inactive. At the end of December, he began to run a high fever and was moved from Kolotichi to Minsk. On examining his wounds, the military doctors discovered that he had developed multiple centres of infection and diagnosed a risk of septicaemia. Georg was therefore condemned to another period of inactivity.

During this time, our regiment, along with its 900 horses, twenty trucks, five tanks and light machine guns, was transferred to the Petrikov sector on the Pripyat River, where the Second Army's staff, which Tresckow had headed since November, was located. Tresckow had two main concerns. Firstly, he wanted to keep 'his' cavalry regiment near him: Operation 'Valkyrie' was now ready, and he had to be ready to act at any moment. Secondly, he needed to secure the 80 to 100 kilometres separating him from Army Group South. To be sure, the Rokitno marshes, whose waters did not freeze, formed a kind of natural defence, but they were not impenetrable. Tresckow had at first envisaged making sporadic use of the regiment for impromptu commando actions. But the situation, which had suddenly deteriorated, forced him to accelerate the transfer of the regiment and to mobilize my battalion immediately.

We covered the 250 kilometres by train. On the night of 31 December 1943, the train stopped in the snow. Not a sound, no one around, no lights – just an icy wind, blowing through the forest powdered with frost. It was 11.30 p.m. The closest German defence posts were more than 6 kilometres away, and the men were concerned that there might be a mechanical problem. But soon my order was passed from one car to another: all batteries were to be set up to test the cannons' abilities. At least, that was the official reason given – my boys needed comforting, and this huge fireworks show (as many as twenty-five cannon shots) would please my cavalrymen and dissuade Russian partisans from attacking our convoy. The sector we were coming into looked extremely desolate. In the tireless struggle against the partisans that infested the region, the SS had devastated, massacred and burned down whole villages. A few inhabitants were still holed up in cellars.

On 9 January 1944, the battalion was assigned to repel a Russian breakthrough. The squadron commanded by Lieutenant Hidding, which had been sent to the site and put into the trenches, was supposed to resist, with only sixty men, three squadrons of enemy cavalry equipped with a battery of light machine guns and an anti-tank battery. Russian losses were dreadful but, subjected to a storm of artillery fire, our forces were soon reduced to about forty individuals. Then I arrived with the two other squadrons. Our counter-attack succeeded in less than three-quarters of an hour, thanks to the effectiveness of the machine pistols we had just received. The next day, the fighting was less favourable to us. On the evening of 10 January, I radioed Kolodichi to request 150 men to replace those I had lost over the preceding two days. In the 3rd Cavalry Squadron alone, there were 44 dead. I was wounded again, for the fifth time since the beginning of the war. On 11 January, a plane sent by Tresckow evacuated me to the military hospital in Minsk.

Georg's health and my own became so much a matter of concern that the high command got involved. Georg, whose doctors couldn't keep him in bed, had started riding again too soon. His wounds had reopened, and the loss of blood nearly killed him. At the suggestion of Marshal Busch, the new commander-in-chief of Army Group Centre, we were both transferred to a hospital in Germany. Then began two long months of inactivity, in the hands of calm and vigilant nuns, in a fairy-tale town, in the shadow of the monastery's bronze bell tower. Münstereifel was only a few dozen kilometres away from Heimerzheim. In that little town, which was hardly threatened by air raids, we felt at home, we received visits from our friends and relatives, and the war seemed infinitely far away.

I was able to resume my command in March 1944, after having handed it over for two months to Wilhelm König. Georg remained on bed-rest until Easter 1944.

Two weeks later, still not fully recovered, he set out for Russia. Although he was only twenty-eight, he had to use a cane to walk, and was very emaciated. When he reached the front on 25 April, he went back to work with all his old vigour. In his absence, important details had been neglected, and errors had been committed. He dismissed three officers the day after he arrived. Although he had been promoted to lieutenant-colonel the preceding December, he was no longer the sole master on board. Since February, the 31st Cavalry Regiment had been integrated into a cavalry brigade. It had been decided not to offer the command to Georg, who was not yet thirty, but rather to an experienced cavalryman of forty-one, Baron von Wolff, who was of Baltic origin. The 3rd Cavalry Brigade (two other brigades were constituted at the same time, one in the north and one in the south) was in reality scarcely any stronger than Georg's old regiment. Each brigade had been reduced from three to two regiments, and each regiment from three to two battalions, so that Baron von Wolff commanded only four battalions.

The Dangerous Ride
(July 1944)

In early June 1944, the Russian front seemed for a time to have been stabilized; it was the calm before the storm. But the situation of the Third Cavalry Brigade was hardly enviable. With less than 3,000 men, it was supposed to defend 55 kilometres of the front and guard eighteen bridges, so that it took the supply column ten hours to make its daily deliveries. The administration was deficient, certain specialities were no longer represented, the men were not always well-trained, and especially, at the end of the fifth year of war, the equipment delivered to us was sometimes unusable, like the 300 saddles we received without girths. The invasion of Normandy further aggravated a situation that was already extremely unfavourable to Germany. On 12 June, after the Allies had landed 326,000 soldiers on the coast of France, it was clear that a breakthrough on the Eastern Front was imminent. On 22 June, the Soviets launched a gigantic frontal attack against Army Group Centre; no less than 2.5 million men advanced on German troops that were six times less numerous.

On 26 June, when the situation was extremely critical, Georg left on leave. Known for his devotion, his acute sense of his responsibilities to his men, and his passionate sense of duty, why did he leave the front at a time like that? Faced with the magnitude of the task, had he given up in discouragement? No. For the past eighteen months, Georg had known that collapse was imminent, and he sought only to delay it with the minimum of losses. For the moment, he wanted to devote all his energy to a manoeuvre Tresckow had asked him to carry out. After spending a few hours at Heimerzheim, he said farewell to the family, perhaps with a premonition that he would never see them again. Then he went to Paris, on the fatuous pretext, which was still taken seriously despite the gravity of the military situation, that Lord Wagram, a stallion that belonged to us – he was confiscated by the French a few months later – was running at Longchamp!

In Paris, at 8 p.m. on 3 July, Marshal von Kluge took command of the Western Front. As soon as he arrived, Georg was received by the marshal. He set forth Tresckow's proposal: first, to eliminate Hitler; second, not to oppose the Allies' breakthrough and surrender unconditionally on the Western Front, and then shift the war effort entirely to Russia and prevent Germany from being crushed by the Soviet war machine; third, to make a peace offer to the Allies, for which purpose Georg agreed to go to England. Kluge sharply rejected this proposal on every point, irritated by what he considered Tresckow's irresponsible behaviour: 'It is pointless to offer the Allies points of entry, because their breakthrough is imminent, and the collapse of the Western Front is now only days away!' And it was pointless, he added, to think about going to England: he couldn't find a pilot reliable enough to carry out such a delicate operation while fighting was raging on the shores of the English Channel. Sick at heart, Georg returned to Russia.

In the East, our marshals had a single concern: to simplify the front line. The bulges and indentations had to be removed to facilitate defence and provide a remedy for the shortage of men, which was becoming more and more manifest. The front had to run along straight lines in order to gain hundreds of kilometres and delay the enemy's implacable advance. Hitler had decided, against all strategic requirements, that the positions had to be held at any cost. He declared several particularly exposed cities to be 'fixed strongpoints'. In a few days, the Russians swept the front away and pulverized the supposed strongpoints. In less than three weeks, the German army lost 350,000 men on the Russian front. Within Army Group Centre, the Fourth and Ninth Armies were annihilated, and the Third Armoured Army was scattered in all directions. Of my brother Georg's old 6th Infantry Division, there remained but a few remnants. Only the Second Army, with ten divisions and one cavalry corps, remained more or less intact, but it was still vulnerable. At its head, Henning von Tresckow, still assisted by Schlabrendorff, had succeeded in stopping the enemy and defending positions. But the cavalry brigade was particularly exposed and frequently called upon, for its capacities were ideal for covering a retreat. Georg could have asked to command it, because know-how was needed. Baron von Wolff had been killed during an exercise on 28 June, and my brother's claim to the position was all the stronger because Marshal Busch was arguing for his appointment. But he now had other priorities in mind. He therefore voluntarily remained on the staff, at Tresckow's disposition. The last act of the conspiracy was at hand.

It was in this context that the gamble of 20 July 1944 took place. On 1 July the appointment of Claus von Stauffenberg as head of staff of the Reserve Army gave him access to the Führer. None of the conspirators had ever been able to get so close to the target. On 11 July, Stauffenberg made a first attempt by bringing a bomb into the Berghof in Berchtesgaden. The absence of Himmler and Göring led him not to go through with the attempt, but in Berlin his accomplice General Olbricht had already launched operation 'Valkyrie'. Not without difficulty, this operation was stopped, and the first steps in a coup d'état and the mobilization of troops stationed in Germany were disguised as a simple exercise. On 15 July, Stauffenberg tried again, and again stopped short, for the same reasons. He wouldn't have another chance; if he failed again, operation 'Valkyrie' would inevitably be compromised.

At the beginning of July, I went to Second Army headquarters to say hello to Tresckow. As he said goodbye, he warned me: 'Take care of yourself! We are soon going to need your services!' Georg and I knew that the assassination attempt was about to be made. We knew our roles by heart, but we didn't know exactly what the others were to do. We didn't know what part Stauffenberg would play, or precisely how the assassination in the Führer's headquarters would take place.

This was perfectly normal; to be effective, a conspiracy has to remain compartmentalized.

Georg had assigned me to be ready to discreetly withdraw the equivalent of six squadrons, or 1,200 men from the front. The goal was to transfer them to Berlin just after the assassination, in order to provide security in a sensitive part of the capital. On 14 or 15 July, Georg confirmed these instructions. It was not an order properly so called, because at headquarters he did not have authority over the 31st Cavalry Regiment, and still less over the brigade. That was what made my situation uncomfortable. I had to act on my own initiative, without formal instructions. Obviously, I would be covered by Tresckow if I was asked to explain what I was doing, but it was up to me to determine the exact modalities for the retreat and the transfer of troops. The operational situation of the Second Army, which was threatened on all sides, was totally unpredictable. Therefore I had to improvise and work against the clock. Providing 1,200 men was not an easy task!

On 6 July, the Second Army's Twentieth Corps had been ordered to retreat. The brigade, aided by a few Hungarian hussars, was supposed to cover the retreat of parts of the infantry. From 11 July on, my regiment was constantly engaged with the enemy north of the two ground links – the road and the rail line – between Pinsk, which had just been evacuated, and Brest-Litovsk. Georg followed these operations with extreme vigilance; he was obsessed by the desire to prevent his cavalrymen from being caught in a trap. At 4 a.m. on 16 July, my regiment arrived in Dohoty, after having ridden half the night. At 8 a.m., Dohoty was attacked again by Russian forces very superior in number to ours. Soviet fighter planes constantly streaked across the sky, while we had no air cover at all. It was no longer a question of whether we should retreat, but how. The next day, this catastrophic scenario began all over again.

On 15 July, I had taken the precaution of withdrawing a squadron of 200 men from the front. They had already started for Berlin. I told the brigade's second-in-command about the withdrawal of these men from combat, and later had great difficulty in explaining their reappearance – which was necessary, however, in order to acquire sufficient provisions. I claimed that I had written one too many zeroes ... For although twenty soldiers can easily appear or disappear, the same does not go for a whole squadron.

I then requisitioned the five additional squadrons we had in mind for operation 'Valkyrie' to assemble in the morning, near Rybno, 8 kilometres south-east of the town of Kobryn. These were three of the four squadrons under my command, and two of Captain Gollert-Hansen's. On 18 July, after giving the units a short rest, we distributed munitions and food supplies for two days and set out. The officers were very surprised, for these marching orders cancelled others that they had received only hours earlier.

The administrative officer of the 3rd Cavalry Brigade, Lieutenant Gigas, saw to it that the Army Group Centre put forty large-capacity trucks at our disposal. Gigas knew enough about the plot to realize that this directive had to be carried out perfectly, but he did not know about the assassination itself. The trucks were to assemble at Konopka. From there they would carry about 1,000 men, piled under tarps, towards an aerodrome in the former Poland. Then they would immediately fly to Berlin's Tempelhof airport. Finally, they would go to Prinz-Albert-Strasse and Wilhelmstrasse, where they would take control of the buildings occupied by the State Security Police and the Ministry of Propaganda. But first of all, they had to ride on horseback the 200 kilometres from Rybno to Konopka.

How, while the war was in full swing, could one carry out a manoeuvre of this kind without arousing suspicion? How could the withdrawal of so many troops go unnoticed? The fact was that the disintegration of the front was so advanced that battalions and even squadrons were attached to their brigades and to their divisions only with regard to logistics and supply. From an operational point of view, the basic units, which were supposed to constitute a self-sufficient point of resistance to the enemy's advance, were put under the control of an Army corps commander. This abbreviated chain of command short-circuited all the intermediate levels. Moreover, in the chaotic retreat, squadrons, detachments, and even patrols were operating in a largely autonomous way. The movements of the cavalrymen thus took place without either the brigade commander or the regimental commander being informed. They were all the less surprised by this momentary disappearance because it had been planned to withdraw the cavalry from the front to Brest-Litovsk, and to hold it in reserve.

Furthermore, the cavalry's tactic of defence and retreat

provided us with good cover. The retreat in fact took place through the successive movements of three lines. The first line (a-c) was supposed to reconnoitre, sometimes far behind the front, and to purge the sector of partisans. It began setting up a retreat position (digging trenches, camouflaging artillery pieces, cutting down pine trees to make fortifications, running barbed wire, etc.). A second line (d-e), about 3 to 5 kilometres behind the front, laid mines, drew up a chart of them, and prepared to blow up bridges and roads at the most critical points. The third line (f-g), was the only one engaged in defensive combat. When it had to retreat, the second line of defence, well installed in its entrenched positions, could in turn resist the enemy assault. The troops withdrawn from the front then established a new line a-c, and so on. Thus it was usual to see units leaving the combat zone and galloping a few kilometres toward the rear.

The remnants of the 31st Regiment covered the infantry's retreat. When the latter had established a new line of defence, I withdrew all my cavalrymen from the front. At my last operations command post, I had received a green light from Georg: 'To Berlin!' I took the car and during the night caught up with the squadrons on their way to Brest-Litovsk. The cavalrymen continued on their way for a day and a night without dismounting. Some of them, beyond exhaustion, fell asleep in the saddle and slipped to the ground . . . The lingering effects of my wounds prevented me from riding for hours and hours. Thus I sometimes directed the movement of the three squadrons, and sometimes reconnoitred by vehicle.

Georg joined us and took command of the three squadrons. Brest-Litovsk had been designated as a fixed strongpoint. We had great difficulty in traversing the city without being requisitioned like every other unit that turned up there. Georg informed me by radio that he had managed to overcome the obstacles put in his way by the commandant of the place, and I was able to take my troops around the city on the north side. My brother then returned to be with Tresckow.

Apart from Georg and me, only two officers had been told what the ultimate goal of our manoeuvre was: König – who had already been involved in the failed attempt made in March 1943 – and the head of the Third Squadron, Captain Hidding. The others who participated in this exhausting ride learned the secret only after the war. One detail, however, had surprised people: I had myself given the order to keep the horses at a trot when crossing cities. For a horseman, trotting on pavement is heresy, because the horses' shoes slip and put both riders and mounts in danger. A few officers thus suspected something unusual, but they kept quiet about it. As the cavalrymen were crossing Brest-Litovsk, they rounded a corner and came face to face with Georg. They expected to be scolded, but he just shouted at them: 'Faster, faster!' The men thought something very special must be going on.

We finally reached the village of Lachovka at around 3 p.m. on 20 July. I gave orders for the units to be reorganized and loaded on the trucks. The horses were to stay where they were, under the guard of a few dozen men. In combat situations, the ratio was normally four horses per guardian; this time it rose to ten horses per guardian – another indication, for the most observant, that this was an exceptional operation.

While I was resting a few moments in the shade of a birch tree, I was surprised to see my brother's regimental postmaster coming toward me. Sergeant Retel was a dedicated communist, but the whole regiment liked him. He handed me a paper on which Georg had scribbled this message: 'Everyone to the old foxholes!' This was a code that meant that the assassination had not been carried out.

There was not a moment to lose. We immediately got back in the saddle and set out in the opposite direction, at the same breakneck speed, toward the front line, which had in the interim moved closer to us. It was only that evening that we heard on the radio about the failure of the assassination attempt and the catastrophe of the unsuccessful coup d'état. In the glum silence punctuated by the clip-clop of the horses's hooves, I had plenty of time for reflection. I was obsessed by one question: was it still really necessary to carry out this assassination? Stauffenberg had asked the same question of Tresckow a few days before the attempt. Why should one risk one's life, and especially that of dozens of other people, when the military situation suggested that in a few months the dictatorship would be over? Tresckow responded forthrightly, as usual: 'The assassination has to take place, whatever the cost. Even if it doesn't succeed, we have to try. Now it is no longer the object of the assassination that matters, but rather to show the whole world and History that the German resistance movement dared to gamble everything, even at the risk of its own life. All the rest, in the end, is merely secondary.'

I took a dim view of my future. The connection between the ride of the 1,200 and the conspiracy that had been discovered was much too obvious not to put Georg and me in danger. Soon I would be asked to account for what I'd done, and it would be very difficult to explain our 400-kilometre ride, especially since it had not been without losses. During the night of 19 July, in fact, I had stopped my car along the road a little to the north-west of Brest-Litovsk: I was watching the cavalry units file by, monitoring the condition of the animals and the men. Then I heard in the distance the sound of a mine exploding. Generally speaking, the explosion of a mine, whose force is largely absorbed by the belly of the mount, killed the horse but only wounded the rider's legs. This time, Captain Hidding had been killed instantly. However, his squadron brought up the end of the column; a thousand men had passed over the same place before him. I raced back along the column. I had to inspect the victim's body as soon as possible, not only because he was a friend, but especially because he carried the maps of Berlin on which were marked in red pencil the areas that we were to seize, the itinerary from Tempelhof, etc. These bits of evidence could not be allowed to fall into anyone's hands but my own. The body would be searched, because it was usual to send personal effects and valuables (medals, watches, wedding rings, signet rings, etc.) to the family of the deceased. Hidding was lying by the wayside; I approached the body and was able to keep others away on the pretext that I wanted to pray. Hunched over the cadaver, almost in contact with his disfigured face, I slipped my hand into his map bag, which was sticky with sweat and blood. I was able to extract the documents, which I hastily stuck inside my shirt. Then I allowed Hidding's orderly to proceed as usual in such cases. I had his coffin loaded onto a truck, with the hope of taking it back to Germany.[21]

At the same time, another incident cost us still more dearly. As well as the forty trucks promised by Army Group Centre, Captain Gigas had provided fifteen additional trucks, with thirty drivers and thirty men to accompany them. But around Brest-Litovsk, the military police diverted the convoy and made it go around the city on the north side. Unfortunately, it was ambushed by Russian tanks and cavalrymen, who had succeeded in making a breakthrough without the Germans' knowledge. Fourteen trucks and about fifty men were captured. One of the trucks managed to get away and was eventually abandoned, the men scattering in the surrounding wheatfields. One soldier thought he'd found a way to save himself by jumping on board a freight train that was passing nearby. But he quickly realized that the cars, which were not under control – one of the engineers had been killed and the other wounded – were rolling toward a burning station where they would end up being fired upon by a Soviet tank. The clandestine passenger jumped off the train and managed to get back to the German positions by passing through the fields.

The panic that reigned over the front was such that no one had really noticed the temporary disappearance of the various squadrons. During the rout, units often lost contact with each other. Sometimes an entire battalion was surrounded and destroyed. They were very happy to see 1,200 men appear – they constituted, after all, about 10 per cent of the brigade's troops.

This was no time for explanations. Officers could not be harassed when maximum operational effectiveness was being asked of them. Therefore Major Brinckmann, who commanded the regiment, did not ask me any questions.

A Time for Mourning

Shortly after 20 July, Georg was named commander of the 3rd Cavalry Brigade. The responsibilities that awaited him were crushing and left no time for gloomy thoughts. In theory, he had under his command 11,500 men, the same number of horses, and a thousand Cossack cavalrymen as auxiliaries. In reality, he lacked more than 2,200 men, 200 auxiliaries, and about a third of the planned equipment.

The battle raged all through the month of August. One incident almost cost Georg his life when he arrived at his new post. He had gone out early in the morning with his communist driver. The road from the Second Army's headquarters to the brigade was considered secure, but their car was ambushed by the Russians. The two men immediately abandoned their vehicle, crossed a little prairie under fire, and took refuge in the undergrowth. Georg saw a murky pond covered with dead leaves and plant debris, in which the roots of several large trees formed natural hiding places. Georg and his reluctant driver entered the muddy water up to their chins and stayed there motionless. Beating the thickets with the butts of their rifles, firing point-blank into copses, the Russians searched for them in vain. Later in the morning, they came back with dogs, which were unable to locate the two men in the malodorous swamp. The afternoon came, and everything seemed calm; birds were warbling. The driver started to move out of the water, but Georg held him back. As an experienced hunter, he had noticed that the birdsong was imitated with bird whistles. They had to wait until the Russians got tired, gave up their search, and left the area at nightfall. Georg wanted at all costs to avoid falling into their hands. In the context of the period after 20 July, his disappearance and captivity by the enemy would have caused him to be seen as a traitor, and it would have directed the authorities' attention towards me, along with questions regarding the true nature of our ride toward the west. Major Kuhn, the operations officer for the 28th Chasseurs Division, who also participated in the conspiracy and was also engaged to a member of Stauffenberg's family, had gone over to the enemy as soon as the failure of the assassination attempt became known. His desertion was interpreted as a simple capture,[22] but a second case would have revealed this disguised escape for what it was.

The following weeks were depressing. The disintegration of the front continued as the beautiful, sunny summer wore on. One piece of terrible news after another reached me in the course of conversations. First Eberhard von Breitenbuch told me that Tresckow had died, immediately after the failure of the assassination attempt. Breitenbuch was the liaison officer for General Model, who had been made commandant of Army Group Centre a few weeks earlier. On the morning of 21

July, a car with a driver was posted in front of the Ostrow barracks, the seat of the Second Army command. Breitenbuch stood near the vehicle, waiting for Tresckow. He had known Tresckow well in his earlier functions, and he wanted to say goodbye to him. When Tresckow appeared, he was calm, relaxed, completely imbued with that inner balance that shaped his appearance. The sunshine seemed to herald a beautiful day – perhaps a little warm. Tresckow smiled at Breitenbuch. The young captain, who had heard about the failed assassination attempt very late the preceding night, excused himself for not being able to accompany his superior officer to the front, where the 28th Rifle Regiment was located, beause he had an assignment to carry out for General Model. He saw a flash of disappointment in Tresckow's eyes: 'Too bad. I would have liked you to witness my death.'

'But you're not going to . . .'

'Yes, I am. I don't want to let our enemies have the satisfaction of taking my life as well.'

He had made everything ready: the pretence of an enemy ambush, the submachine gun he would be holding, the grenade that he would press against his belly. Tresckow told the distraught Breitenbuch what he wanted to happen afterwards. Then, still just as tranquilly, he shook his hand firmly. 'Goodbye. We will see each other in a better world.' Tresckow got into the car, which then drove away, taking to his death the soul of this vast conspiracy in which Oster had been the brain, Beck the spinal marrow, and Stauffenberg the arm bearing the weapon. On 21 July,

Tresckow had sent his wife a farewell letter[23] disguised as an ordinary note. A few days earlier, he had sent his cherished Erika a newspaper clipping of this poem:

> A man who can keep his childhood dreams in all their
>   purity,
> Preserving them in his naked and defenseless breast,
> Who, despite the laughter of this world, dares to live as
>   he had dreamed in his childhood,
> Down to his last day: yes, that is a man, a man in all he
>   is.

At first, Tresckow's death was so well camouflaged that people believed that he had in fact been killed in a lethal skirmish with partisans. His body was taken back to Germany and buried with military honours on the family estate of Wartenberg. But all the lines of investigation into the assassination attempt pointed to him. Sometime around the middle of August, the SS came to dig up and dispose of the body; Tresckow's widow and his daughters were already either in prison or in a foster home.

Helmut Stieff was one of the first arrested and put to death. Already on 20 July, fearing that the attempt would fail, he had acted in a way that was not in accord with the second part of operation 'Valkyrie': his indecisiveness had marked him as guilty. Betrayed by his contradictions, he was tortured and had confessed, but had fingered only people who were already dead. He was executed on 8 August, hanged with one of the piano strings that had prolonged his suffering under torture.

Hans-Ulrich von Oertzen, whose role was to take over an area of Berlin, was put under arrest two days after the attempt and interrogated by the military. He was only twenty-nine, and had been married for four months. He managed to telephone his young wife one last time, and then, knowing that the Gestapo would arrive at any moment, he pretended that he really had to go, locked himself in the toilet, put a grenade in his mouth, and pulled the pin. His guards, who heard the explosion, found his poor decapitated body among the debris of the door they had smashed in. Heinrich von Lehndorff – the man who had witnessed the massacre at Borissov – was arrested the same day. Sentenced to death on 3 September, he was hanged the next day, leaving a wife and four children behind him. On 26 July, it was Wessel Freytag von Loringhoven's turn to commit suicide. A colonel, forty-four years old, he had provided explosives and this had been discovered. At the same time, Georg Schultze-Büttger was taken into custody. He was hanged on 13 October 1944, a few days after he turned forty.

On 17 August 1944, Fabian von Schlabrendorff was also arrested. Tortured at length by the Gestapo, he did not give us away. 'The Boeselager brothers? No, they're excellent soldiers, completely loyal. They had nothing to do with it. You're wasting your time.' Under torture, his legal training came out. He raised procedural issues and during a hearing he objected to the illegality of the treatment meted out to prisoners. Two of his ribs had been broken while he was being interrogated; he showed the injury in court, creating turmoil, taking aback the prosecution, and causing the trial to be suspended. Then he had a real stroke of luck: the courthouse was bombed, and his judicial dossier was lost in its ruins, along with the presiding judge, the infamous Freisler, who had been carrying it. Asked afterwards why he had been arrested and interned, he replied that he was accused of 'illegally slaughtering cattle'. He was put in a concentration camp and transferred, along with General Halder and former French prime minister Léon Blum, to the South Tyrol. After being freed by American troops, he returned to civilian life and resumed his work as a jurist; in 1967 he was appointed to the German constitutional court (*Bundesverfassungsgericht*). He died in 1980.

The day Schlabrendorff was arrested, Marshal Kluge was relieved of his command. Too much evidence showed that he had known what was going on and had covered for his subordinates: he was virtually condemned. On his way back to Germany, the old soldier committed suicide. He wrote a last letter to the Führer, begging him to stop the war, and declaring his fidelity for the last time. Despite these warnings, the war continued to chew up lives, families and whole cities. On 15 August, it was our dear Wilhelm König, our king of steel, who lost his life. Having survived incredible dangers, as if invulnerable, he was killed in an absurd way. One evening as he sat at his work table he was hit by a stray mortar shell.

Every day, the post brought us new reasons to mourn. Every day, official information reported the progress of summary trials. Hitler was undertaking a systematic purge. The repression spread, extending even to those who had only guessed what the conspirators were doing. Thousands of persons were interned, sometimes for vague relationships with the members of the conspiracy. The military institution had to submit. Political commisars were named for the armies.

On 24 July, the old military salute was abolished and replaced by the Nazi salute. Langen, the secretary of the First Squadron of the 31st Cavalry Regiment, received Göring's order to this effect by telephone. It was effective immediately. He typed up the verbal directive and presented it to the commander of the brigade straight away. It was important enough to warrant interrupting the officers' work session. Georg was conducting a major briefing with the commanders of the two regiments, the battalions, and the different squadrons. Langen, a non-commissioned officer, knocked at the door: 'Colonel, may I come in?'

'Yes, what is it?' Georg asked, somewhat abruptly.

Langen came in and, following the new orders regarding military discipline, clicked his heels and gave the Nazi salute. The officers were appalled. In normal times, they might have smiled or thought it was a joke in poor taste. But in the context of the failed coup d'état, there was nothing to smile about.

'What is wrong with you? What does this mean?' Georg asked severely, showing an irritation that was unusual in him.

Without a word, Langen handed him the paper. After rapidly perusing it, Georg asked: 'Langen, from whom do you usually receive your orders?'

'From you, Colonel, and from the officers of our regiment, naturally,' the non-commissioned officer replied sheepishly.

'Good, Langen, you've understood. You may go,' Georg concluded more kindly, with a slight smile.

The secretary backed out of the room after giving a very martial, and very classic, military salute. The directive was not followed in the brigade. A political commissar was named, but he was a former communist full of contradictions and showed no particular zeal in exercising his office. Moreover, he quickly became the butt of jokes within the brigade.

On 8 August, I was named to head the 41st Regiment of the 2nd Cavalry Brigade, whose commandant had just been seriously wounded. I said goodbye to my brother, my childhood companion, without suspecting that death was soon to separate us forever.

'How many times in the course of this war have I prayed to God to take my life and preserve that of others whom I consider more important than I am! He has not listened to me, because apparently I have not yet passed my qualifying examination in the beyond,' Georg wrote in a letter to Annarès von Wendt in September 1942. Now Georg had passed his exam. He had shown that he could follow his convictions through to the end. In a certain sense, he could perhaps die. In any event, he was ready to die. He was killed in combat on 29 August 1944, on the borders of East Prussia, on the Bug River near Lady-Mans. While he was driving along a ridge from which he was directing the movements of his troops by radio, his vehicle was targeted by enemy mortar fire.

He had just celebrated his twenty-ninth birthday. His participation in the conspiracy remained confidential. His body was taken back to Heimerzheim – this was unusual in the context of the complete collapse of the military situation – and he was given a formal funeral. When Georg died, I lost almost half of myself. Tresckow, Hidding, König, all the members of the conspiracy whom I knew were dead. I was the only one still carrying my secret, without anyone to confide in.

But operational necessities did not leave me time to weep. Every day there was a new Russian attack that nibbled off a few more kilometres. We were defending ourselves inch by inch, but we had to face facts: the Red Army would soon be at the gates of East Prussia. In the second half of August, the forces within which I was exercising my command, which were at that time retreating toward the west near Bialystok, began to move north, toward the border of East Prussia, and provided a clearly marked target for the Soviets.

In late August, I was summoned to Army headquarters. A plane was supposed to take me there on 1 September. This was clearly a trap to take me into custody. I was certain that my end was near. In a state of deep anxiety, I ran toward the plane, whose engines were already humming. My travelling Bible dropped out of my poorly closed bag and fell open. I bent down to pick it up, and saw these lines of the Benedictus: *Ut sine timore, de manu inimicorum nostrorum liberati, serviamus illi.*[24]

I regained my confidence and got into the plane, saying to myself: 'By the grace of God!'

The Bridge over the Mura
(1945)

It was not a trap that awaited me at Army headquarters, but an appointment as special officer for the cavalry. I thus became the staff's correspondent for all matters connected with the mounted cavalry, and responsible for equipment, and for the distribution and numbers of these troops, whether regarding the two brigades of mounted cavalry, the cavalry units attached to reconnaissance battalions for infantry divisions, cyclist units, or the cavalry training school. I received requests from the operational units and dealt with them in coordination with various administrative entities. I frequently went into the field, travelling along the front lines at the wheel of my car, in order to forge my own opinion concerning the most difficult points. The rest of the time I was located, like a large part of the infantry staff, in the offices of the former school of athletics in Wünsdorf.[25] Since the town was more than 50 kilometres outside Berlin, it was rarely bombarded. But this period was nonetheless anxiety-producing. Not allowing myself to confide in anyone, to avoid aggravating my situation or endangering those with whom I might have spoken, I expressed myself freely only with my orderly. The atmosphere of feigned camaraderie among the staff was rather overdone;

everyone watched what he said, while avoiding a reserve that would have been too suspect. But I sometimes found it too hard to contain my feelings.

I had been invited by Burgdorf – Hitler's aide-de-camp and the head of his personal office – who at that time called the shots at headquarters, to an 'after-dinner wine-tasting'. There were many generals there, and I was by far the youngest guest. Towards the end of the evening, as I was getting ready to go, I heard Burgdorf say in the next room: 'When the war is over, we will have to purge, after the Jews, the Catholic officers in the Army.' I went into the room and after thanking him in the usual way, I said: 'As a Catholic officer, I found what you just said very informative, General. I'd like you to know that despite my flaws, I have served the German people at the front, I have been wounded five times, and been awarded the Iron Cross.' There was an embarrassed silence, and without staying any longer I politely took my leave.

As for my new assignment, while I was sorry to give up operational functions and leave my men to their fate, I gained an overall view and an influence that I had never had before. I quickly became convinced that despite the distance, I could still be indirectly useful to my men. Over the following months, I had only one pre-occupation: to save as many cavalrymen as I could. Until October, my former companions in arms were used in inappropriate ways, broken up into minuscule units in an extremely lethal trench warfare on the borders of East Prussia. The number of horses at their disposal declined drastically. My visits in the field confirmed my worst fears. With the rapid advance of the Red Army, East Prussia was in danger of being surrounded and the troops that were protecting it were threatened with complete annihilation. I wanted to get my comrades out of this wasp's nest, and to do so I counted on the Führer's craziest plans. For the end of 1944, Hitler envisaged a gigantic offensive far to the south, through Romania, in order to strike the oil wells in the Caucasus. The cavalry, which was very mobile, was ideally suited to this kind of operation: that was the argument I did not scruple to use in order to move my cavalrymen to a less dangerous theatre of operations ...

Colonel von Bonin was at that time head of the operations division of the General Staff; he supported my plan. In addition, through the intermediary of his orderly, I had Guderian's ear. On 28 November 1944, the 3rd Cavalry Brigade received its evacuation order and left a front where it had lost, in less than two years, forty-six officers, 850 non-commissioned officers and regular troops, and had more than 3,600 wounded. It took the last trains to get out of East Prussia. It took no less than fifty-six convoys to transport men, equipment, and horses. During the second half of December, the troops arrived in Hungary, near Lake Balaton, amid vineyards, ancient churches and abbeys, and manor houses from the Austro-Hungarian period. This rolling landscape seemed particularly cheering after the rigours of the devastated Russian plain. But the Soviets were already there. The Führer's offensive was no more than a madman's dream, and we could hope to do no more than delay the enemy's advance.

When I was finally able to rejoin my beloved cavalrymen, the Red Army was already at the gates of Austria. In the meantime, I had been promoted to the rank of major, and I was put in command of the 31st Cavalry Regiment. I was welcomed with a joy that did my heart good, despite the difficulties which still faced us.

The news of Hitler's death reached the troops on 1 May 1945. It was met with general indifference, even among his former supporters: for months, everyone had been thinking only about getting home alive. My sole concern was to ensure that the boys who had been entrusted to me would return to Germany. Until the last day, I had all the infirmaries in the region searched for the division's wounded and amputated men, in order to spare them from being massacred should the sector be taken over by Tito's partisans or by the Red Army. I did the impossible, right under the noses of the Russians, whose drunkenness helped me get three wounded officers out of the Judenburg hospital.

I heard about the armistice on the night of 8 May 1945, when the cavalry division had just finished its last hunting party of the war – and of its history. We had to make the right decisions, because the armistice did not mean the end of hostilities. The Russians were taking advantage of this unstable period to seize as much territory as possible. Our regiment was supposed to cover the retreat of the whole cavalry corps, whose first units had crossed the Mura, south of Graz, on 7 May. On 9 May, shortly after midnight, at the rear of the cavalry corps, I myself crossed the bridge at Wildon.

In the moonlight, I stopped my horse for a moment and went over to the parapet. Plunging two fingers into the lining of the left pocket of my uniform jacket, I pulled out the little cyanide capsule that had been with me for almost three years. Kluge, whose son-in-law was a doctor, had given it to me one day when our airplane was almost shot down by partisans. I threw it into the river. Thus this symbol of the painful end of my youth, of those years of bitterness and dread, of unspoken fears, sank silently into the water. This poison capsule was death itself, caught in a fold of my garment. I felt lighter. The war was over. I was alive!

But this was no time for dreaming. The roads were crowded with cars, trucks, and armoured vehicles of all kinds. I had the bridge blown up at 4.30 a.m., in order to slow the Russians' advance a little. In Wildon, I demanded that the mayor immediately burn the red flags adorned with the hammer and sickle that the inhabitants, who had two months earlier been supporters of Germany, had been cowardly enough to hang from the windows of their houses. When evening came, we set up our headquarters in the village of Weitenhof, where we rested. The Mura, more than 8 kilometres away, marked the boundary between the Russian and the Allied zones. We thought we were safe there, but we were mistaken. We had hardly settled in before my driver shouted: 'The Russians are here with tanks!' In a moment, we evacuated the village, the staff cars roaring off right in front of the stunned Russians, and we took the road to Köflach. At some distance from the town, the head of the column called me on the radio: 'Commandant, the English are in front of us. What should we do?'

'Well, say hello to them!'

I went up to the head of the column in order to meet my British counterpart. The introductions were cordial. We exchanged cigarettes. I told the Englishman that the Russians were occupying Graz. 'Don't you want to help us drive them out?' he asked.

'No thanks, frankly. Since the armistice, my job is to take my regiment back to Paderborn, in Germany.'

To escape the crowded roads and at the risk of running into the Russians, we branched off to the west, and led by a guide, took a mountain road. It was there that we had arranged to stay when the English accepted our capitulation on 11 May. We were supervised by cavalrymen, or rather former cavalrymen who had been transformed into tank men.

The countryside was splendid, and nature seemed to have prepared herself carefully to welcome our exhausted soldiers and provide rest for them. The solemn setting of the Alps, the pine forests, the flourishing vegetation in full bloom – everything contributed to give the surrounding mountains an unreal appearance. The fighting, the gunshots, the machine-gun fire, the attackers' wild cries, and the death rattles of the dying quickly became memories. After having lived in the depths of Hell, we were now near Heaven. Game was abundant – roedeer and woodcocks delighted hunters. We had to find activities to occupy men who suddenly found themselves with nothing to do: I took volunteers on long rambles on horseback high into the mountains, we organized equestrian tournaments, Roman chariot races, and even acted out the rape of the Sabines in period costumes. We were not taken prisoner or even completely disarmed. By July, I was home again, my pistol in my belt and flanked by my two horses.

Epilogue

One day in October 2003, I received a letter from the office of the French minister for European Affairs, inviting me to a meeting with members of the French resistance that was to be held early in the following year, in the presence of a few hundred secondary school students. On the occasion of the sixtieth anniversary of the invasion of Normandy, France also wanted to highlight the sixtieth anniversary of the assassination attempt made on 20 July. The presence of the last witness of the resistance to Hitler among the German military was supposed to serve the cause of Franco-German friendship.

I accepted on the condition that I not be given a starring role. I was only the last representative of those whom fate had treated less generously. I therefore insisted on being accompanied by Tresckow's daughter, General von Hammerstein-Equordt's daughter, and Hans Oster's daughter-in-law – who herself had been arrested in April 1943 for collaborating with the lawyer Müller, who was conscientiously passing information to the Allies through a religious pipeline. The meeting took place on 27 January 2004, in a venue filled with sinister memories: the Foreign Ministry's Kleber conference centre in the former Hotel Majestic, whose cellars had been used to torture members of the resistance. On the platform were Jacques Baumel, Marie-Jo Chombart de Lowe, Jean Gavard, Lucie Aubrac, and also Uta von Aretin, Anna Oster, and myself. This was a very moving moment for me.

Moreover, France had reserved for me an unexpected honour: I was made an officer of the Legion d'honneur, as a posthumous homage to all my companions, and to Tresckow in particular. This gesture, carried out by France's minister for European Affairs, was full of great symbolic value. The next day, I went to the Arc de Triomphe to lay a wreath on the tomb of the Unknown Soldier. This was a kind of vengeance taken on cruelty and incomprehension for a man like me who had always tried to follow three rules: to keep my political conscience awake, to respond to the call, and also to know how to say no.

Philipp von Boeselager agreed to participate in long conversations about the period that provided the subject matter for this book. He did not like to talk about these events. Every reference to them elicited memories that were almost always cruel, and filled with suffering as well. His participation in the plots against Hitler was a difficult secret to bear during the war and afterwards. He did not talk about it, at first, even to his wife. But at the time of writing he was the last of the conspirators who was still alive. And since he did not believe in chance, he knew that if he had survived, it was in order to testify.

Were it not for a few traces of the wounds he received in combat, one would never guess that this old man, who radiated an impression of inner peace, had experienced the interminable nightmare of the Second World War. Nor, especially, that he lived in a state of perpetual internal tension resulting from his participation in the conspiracies against Hitler. To be a conspirator was to plan a crime. In the eyes of other Germans, it was to betray one's country and hasten its final destruction. It was, finally, to lead a double life, a difficult task for a man who had been brought up to follow the code of chivalry.

To mention Philipp von Boeselager here without also mentioning his brother Georg would be a nonsense. They were inseparable in their childhood games and in the rigours of the war, and they both carried the secret of the conspiracy. No doubt they did so out of a sense of duty, a way of being and thinking that is illustrated by another episode, anecdotal with respect to history, but which also explains how I came to be involved in co-writing this book.

Shortly before the beginning of the offensive against the Soviet Union in 1941, Antonius and Georg von Boeselager, along with my grandfather Karl von Wendt,[26] made a friendly pact: if one of them died during the war, the others would somehow find a way to bring his body back to Germany. This strange agreement soon had to be put into effect, alas, when Antonius died during the first weeks of the conflict. In November 1941, when Georg sent Karl von Wendt to look for warm clothing in Germany, he asked him to make a detour to Welish: under cover of night, he was supposed to disinter Tonio and take his body back to Heimerzheim. Karl did not demur; he did what was asked of him. When he arrived in Heimerzheim in the middle of the night, he dug a grave in the castle's private cemetery and buried the body.

In August 1942, Karl in turn died during the violent fighting around Rzhev. Georg, who was then in Romania, could do nothing. Then, starting in January, he was too occupied with the reorganization of the cavalry. So he entrusted the operation to Philipp, who was still Marshal von Kluge's aide-de-camp. Philipp had the staff's carpenter construct an oblong box lined with zinc, which was supposed to protect his maps from the damp. The explanation seemed plausible enough; the box didn't really look like a coffin. Accompanied by his orderly, Philipp went to the cemetery where Karl had been buried. It was toward the end of the winter. Time was limited, because the Russian pressure on Rzhev was increasing again, and the region would no doubt have to be abandoned, along with its cemeteries containing many of their comrades. The two men went as far as Grubewo, 5 kilometres from the city. The incessant combats over the winter had transformed the countryside into a lunar landscape. Of the city, which formerly had 57,000 inhabitants, there remained only ruins. That night, they went into the cemetery. The cross on top of the tomb, with its inscription still perfectly legible, rose over a thick layer of snow. They brushed the snow off the tomb, but the ground was completely frozen. They had to sprinkle gasoline on the ground and set it on fire. It was a strange sight – these flames flaring in the quiet of a snowed-in cemetery, amid the silent population of ghosts! Philipp and his orderly didn't linger. They transferred the body to the map box, locked it, refilled the hole, and left. A few days later, Rzhev fell into Russian hands.

However, neither Philipp nor Georg had time to return to Germany. The military situation was poor. Philipp's new responsibilities did not allow him to go on leave. Therefore he kept the body with him. The box was equipped with handles that made it easier to load on trucks. During sedentary periods, the mysterious container was unloaded and put in Philipp's lodging or his tent. He travelled for no less than eighteen months with Karl's body, which was finally buried only in mid August 1944, by his brother-in-law Kaspar von Fürstenberg, a few days after Philipp took command of the 41st Cavalry Regiment. Philipp's efforts made it possible to rediscover my grandfather's remains and take them home to Germany in August 1997.

BIBLIOGRAPHY AND SOURCES

On resistance within the military:

Hoffmann, Peter, *La Résistance allemande contre Hitler*, Balland, Paris, 1994.

Thun-Hohenstein, Romedio Galeazzo, *Der Verschwörer: General Oster und die Militäropposition*, Severin und Siedler, Berlin, 1982.

On Henning von Tresckow

Henning von Tresckow, *Ich bin, der ich war*, Lukas Verlag, Berlin, 2001.

On Georg von Boeselager

Doepgen, Heinz W. Georg von, *Boeselager. Kavallerie-Offizier in der Militäropposition gegen Hitler*, Herford, Mittler, 1986.

On Army Group Centre and the 6th Infantry Divison in particular:

Grossmann, *Geschichte der rheinisch-westfälischen 6. Infante-rie-Division 1939-1945*, Hans-Henning Podzun Verlag, Bad Nauheim, 1958.

Haape, Dr Heinrich, *Endstation Moskau 1941–1942*, Motor-buch Verlag, 1998. A very detailed and lively account of the beginning of the Russian campaign, written by the doctor of the 3rd Battalion of the 18th Infantry Regiment of the 6th Division. With maps and illustrations.

Kurowski, Franz, *Die Heeresgruppe Mitte*, Podzun-Pallas Verlag, Wölfersheim, 2001.

On the German Cavalry and the Boeselager brothers

Witte, Hans-Joachim et Offermann, Peter, *Die Boe-selagerschen*
Reiter, Das Kavallerie-Regiment Mitte und die aus ihm her-vorgegangene 3. Kavallerie-Brigade, Schild Verlag, 1998.

On the attitude of a non-commissioned officer during the Russian campaign

Fehrenbach, Florence, *Un coeur allemand* – Karl von Wendt (1911–1942), un catholique d'une guerre à l'autre, Privat, Toulouse, 2006.

Kageneck, August von, *Examen de conscience*, Perrin, Paris, 1996.

Kageneck, August von, *Lieutenant de Panzer*, Perrin, Paris, 1994.

Notes

[1] This residence was sold to the municipal government in 1923.

[2] Although the Republican constitution secularized education, primary education remained de facto under the supervision of the clergy.

[3] I did not personally experience this episode, because at that time I was several hundred kilometres away. But my brother told me about it. Moreover, the following sequence has been described in the 6th Division's journal of operations.

[4] The 86th Division's movements were, after the sickle-shaped sweep toward the English Channel, part of the German General Staff's other great strategic manoeuvre intended to cut up and disorganize the French defence.

[5] Karl von Wendt, an officer under Georg's command, comments on the attitude of the French people he had been able to observe in the town where Georg was in charge: 'What is most surprising is that in both their behaviour toward us and in their way of life, there was no sign that the French had lost the war to us. In the long run, they will finally realize this. It is equally strange to see so few people mourning, even though we can assume that every family has sustained a loss. However, we hear many people say that they are in captivity in Germany. But since these prisoners provide very favourable reports regarding the manner in which they are treated in Germany, the population is very friendly and helpful to us. People never cease to go into ecstasies over the fact that we are very decent boys, and they do not hesitate to express very clearly their admiration for our army. In particular, they are astonished by the quality of our discipline, and they put the blame for their defeat

wholly on the poor leadership of the French armies.' Quoted in Florence Fehrenbach, *Un coeur allemand*.

[6] This is once again corroborated by Karl von Wendt, Georg's faithful battalion chonicler, in a letter written to his wife on 20 July 1941, in the heat of action: 'The Russian people reject this war more and more as we advance, and themselves call the Russian Army "Bolsheviks", with whom they have no relationship. In many places we see people bringing their crosses and icons out of hiding places; many of the prisoners display religious medals to prove their good faith when we ask whether they are Bolsheviks. Hardly a day goes by without people among the civilian population, usually older people, telling us that communists are still hiding in the forests. Obviously, we can't go running after every one of them, but I think the civilian population is 70 per cent on our side. In particular, when they have lived a few days alongside German soldiers and have been able to see that we aren't killers and brigands like the Reds, who behave in a truly crazy way within their own country. In the long run, the Russians would not be able to maintain that kind of regime, and the game will soon be up for the Reds who are holding power. May the Lord be merciful if they fall into the hands of this people whom they have persecuted for twenty years now. The few cities and towns that there are here are now being systematically burned by the Reds, but that does not harm us or put us in danger, only it will take the country a long time to rebuild itself.' (Ibid.)

[7] These were 75 mm mortars, adapted so that they could be pulled by horses at a trot. They had a limited range.

[8] Since 1938, Oster had been risking his life in an effort to bring together undecided generals in order to lead them to undertake a putsch and prevent a war that would be disastrous for Germany – the Abwehr had understood this as early as the mid 1930s – because the country did not have, any more than it had had in 1914, the resources to sustain a long war. Several times, he had purely and simply committed treason, handing over to the Western powers information regarding war plans and communicating to the Dutch military attaché, on 8 May 1940, the date the offensive was to begin.

[9] Letter to Anna-Therese Freifrau von Wendt, 5 October 1942.

[10] Letter to Anna-Therese Freifrau von Wendt, 12 October 1942.

[11] In 1924, he had been expelled from the Reichswehr because of his pro-Nazi sympathies. After half a decade of struggling to survive in one job after another, he received a large inheritance. He joined the Nazi party in 1930, the SS in 1931, and became a deputy to the Reichstag in 1932.

[12] In 1942, he fell into a deep depression that left him at the edge of madness. Bach-Zelewski both conceived and centralized the battle against partisans, and he was also an advocate of recourse to 'the most brutal means'. On this subject, see J.-L. Leleu, *La Waffen SS*, Perrin, Paris, 2007, pp. 788-95. We can imagine that Kluge at least knew what kind of man he was dealing with.

[13] Bach-Zelewski died in 1972, after ten years in prison.

[14] Stargard (in Polish, Starogard) had been given to Poland in May 1920 along with the Polish Corridor, and reincorporated into Prussia in November 1939 after the destruction of Poland.

[15] The Wolfschanze, near Rastenburg in East Prussia, is the best known and the best organized of the different general headquarters. The one in Vinnytsia (Wehrwolf) was used from July to October 1942.

[16] Böhne was an estate belonging to the Marshal von Kluge's wife.

[17] Bernd von Kleist was then an administrative officer (Ib) on the staff.

[18] The story told by the non-commissioned officer Heetman expresses the admiration and even affection that his men felt for their leader, which is also proven by the use of the nickname [Schorsch = Georg]: 'Yes, our Schorsch is coming to visit his good old squadron. We all like him and venerate him, and we would follow him into Hell. We can hardly control our impatience. While waiting, we've all gathered, some at his post, others in front of his bunker. No one is cold, despite the Siberian cold, because our Schorsch is going to arrive. And then, suddenly, like a hunter on the lookout for game, there he is in front of us, accompanied by our King of iron and steel. He smiles at us, shakes our hands, and talks to us the way a father talks to his children. He knows how much we are suffering, he knows that things are going badly for us. He

talks about the future. Everything is silent, we hang on his every word. He is going to get us out of here and put together a cavalry group. At the mere thought of that, all the cavalrymen's hearts swell in their breasts. Then he shakes everyone's hand again, wishes us good luck, and bids us farewell.' Quoted by Hans-Joachim Witte and Peter Offermann, *Die Boeselagerschen Reiter: Das Kavallerie-Regiment Mitte und die aus ihm hervorgegangene 3. Kavallerie-Brigade*, Schild Verlag, 1998, p. 23.

[19] After the war, Hans Herwarth von Bitterfeld became the German ambassador in London and a secretary of state to President Lübke.

[20] It is impossible to say with certainty whether it was these explosives that he used in the following days. It seems, in fact, that Stauffenberg had explosives that came from at least four different sources, only two of which were discovered by the Gestapo. The precautions taken at every step of the way prevented the investigators from reconstituting the whole sequence

[21] Hidding was finally interred about 16 August 1944, a month after his death, along the road to Jedrejzow, at the same place as the grandfather of Florence Fehrenbach.

[22] Major Kuhn survived his captivity in Russia, but returned to Germany in very poor condition.

[23] Born Erika von Falkenhayn, she was the daughter of the German general who started the battle of Verdun in 1916 and was defeated by the British in Palestine in 1917. Since his leave in 1943, she had been aware of what her husband was doing.

[24] Luke, 1:73: 'that we, being delivered from the hand of our enemies/ might serve Him without fear.'

[25] On the outskirts of Zossen, the town of Wünsdorf had been since 1908 the home of an Army training centre, which became the Army's official School of Athletics in 1924.

[26] On Karl von Wendt (1911-1942), his life and his correspondence, see Florence Fehrenbach, *Un coeur allemand*.